SAI BABA

IS STILL ALIVE

Jaya Wahi

Times Group Books

11 Assurances of Sai Baba

The moment you set your feet on the soil of Shirdi, your sufferings will come to a n end.

Those that climb the steps of My Samadhi, shall be blessed with abundance of joy and bliss.

Even though I have given up My physical form, I shall run to My devotees when they call out to Me.

Let your faith unto My feet be ever strong and even when I am gone, My tomb shall fulfil all your desires.

Know Me as ever alive, experience My eternal presence and understand this truth of My soulful existence.

Whoever has come to My door or taken refuge in My feet has never returned empty-handed.

As you believe in Me, so shall you experience My presence and My love.

Cast all your burdens on Me and I shall carry you safely in My arms and never let down your faith.

The wealth of My love is flowing in abundance, your dreams are not far; come and take away as much as you need.

First published in 2013
Seventh reprint April 2017

Times Group Books

A division of
Bennett, Coleman & Co. Ltd.
s of India, 10 Daryaganj, New Delhi-110002
1-39843333, Email: tgb@limcsgroup.in,www.toibooks.com

SAI BABA IS STILL ALIVE

ISBN 978-93-86206-23-7
Price: ₹325

Printed at: SEA Prim (P) Ltd.

This one's for You..

Baba, Maa & Papa ☺

Contents

Foreword

BE A FAKIR AND LIVE IN BLISS

Spirituality for me is a very personal thing. My knowledge of spirituality began by watching my mother and hence, for me my mother is my religion. The way she conducted her life and ran our home was like a lesson in moral science every day. So, when I read about Sal Baba and all that He professed, the one thing that comes to my mind is this: Be a fakir and live in bliss.

Sai Baba was all about giving, even if you had none. And even in my childhood 1 was taught the same — to give and help those less fortunate than you are; because only when you give, do you get. So, reading a saint's teachings should not begin and end with reeling away his thoughts. It's all about feeling the spirit behind those thoughts and then implementing them in your life.

In the little spiritualism that I practice, I've realized that it's important to be good but not so good that you try to become God. Also, it's okay to be bad but not so bad so as to become a devil. If one can just strive to be a good human being to others, we truly can aim to live like THE fakir and so live in bliss too!

JACKIE SHROFF
Mumbai, 2013

Acknowledgements

As I sit down to thank all those people instrumental in bringing forth this book, I am left to wonder, where do I fit in this picture? The complete credits for writing this book go to Baba and I am the one expressing gratitude. ☺ Strange... isn't it?? But fun apart, there truly are a lot of wonderful souls that I need to thank, those that have been a part of Eaba and my beautiful journey through this book.

First and foremost, my pranam and gratitude at the feet of my brother, Lord Ganesha (on Whose wrist I tie the sacred thread of Rakbi year after year since my childhood) and my Lady of Wisdom, Maa Saraswati. My gratefulness to both of You for blessing me with ever-effulgent inner light, so that I could take up this blissful yet arduous task of writing a book on Baba Sai.

Next, a big thank you to my strong yet soft-hearted Dad, Col. Raj Kumar Wahi, and my ever graceful Maa, Sharda Wahi, for bringing rne into this world and imbibing in me virtues, inner goodness and love for the Lord, which are very big reasons that this book has come through me. i am what I am because of your blessings and upbringing. Love you, Paa and Maa. Thank you so much for making me a good girl. © And not to miss my little angel sister Neha, who has been a constant, undiminishing driving force in my life and whose magical dreams of Baba opened our lives and our hearts to His Divine Presence. You complete me, Neha... you truly do!! Love you!! And finally... my princess Saiesha and my sweetheart Gaurav. Love you both from the depth of my heart.... Thanks for making my life and my world beautiful.

I always knew Baba loved me deeply but the biggest testimony of His love for me came as His greatest gift... my husband Kumar. There is no doubt that Baba sent him to this world for me. Most loving, giving, understanding, sacrificing, encouraging... I could go on and on and yet fall short of words to describe him. Thanks, Hubby!! 1 would be nowhere minus your love, teachings and inspiration. Thanks for such faith in me and my abilities. Your faith gives me faith. You have been — and are — the wind beneath my wings. ☺

My book would be incomplete — in fact, hollow and empty — without the gems of wisdom drawn out of the Shri Sai Satcharita. We have not been fortunate enough to meet Baba but the Shri Sai Satcharita abounds with the teachings, lessons and life of Baba Sai. Since, in my belief, the Sai Satcharita is the most authentic book on Baba available to us, I have extensively used quotes and teachings of Baba from the aforesaid, especially at the beginning of the chapters. Baba always taught that His teachings must be shared abundantly and wholesomely. 1 have done the same. ☺ And I extend my deepest gratitude to Shri Govind Raghunath Dabholkar (Hemadpant) and the Shri Sai Baba Sansthan Trust, Shirdi, for giving us this wealth of wisdom. May Baba bless you all with His grace.

And finally, all those wonderful God-sent angels who made my spiritual journey through this book more meaningful and my life more worthy... Una Akbar, my dear friend from London, for being my greatest motivator and for making me believe in myself. Truly love you, soul sister!! My thanks to Sanjay Bhatnagar of Times Group Books, whom Baba has chosen as a channel for this book to reach millions of devotees. Thanks a lot for your faith in me!! And now Madhulita Mohanty, my graceful friend and the National Editor of TGB... this book has come through the Times Group because I loved you and your reassuring smile; a smile which gave me the confidence of handing over my hard work of years into your able hands. 1 loved the faith you expressed in me and my book. Thank you so much!! And last but not the least... my lovely Monali Banerjee, the editor of *Sai Baba Is Still Alive* and now a dear friend too. You truly made my journey more special. Your eye for precision, your innumerable inputs and your undying effort have done wonders for 'our book'. ☺ My most delightful achievement is that you too fell in love with dear Baba during this editing. When we began, you barely knew Baba and today you too live by His name. What sheer joy!! Love you, Monali... thank you!! Keep smiling forever. ☺

Destiny snatched away three brothers but gave back one who loves me as much as all three together would have!! Love you, bro Sunil Tlku. © Don't know what all to thank you for. So for now just thanking you for being there and also for the Cover Page and Pictures in our book. A Big Thank You to Rakesh Dhasmana, Dev Kumawat and Pranav Kaul for creating a Baba out of my dreams and visions. Thank you so much for ensuring that Baba's eyes, full of love, and His smile reach devotees across the world. I appreciate the endless hours and the selfless effort behind the beautiful creations. Baba bless you all.

My final word of gratitude to those children of Baba, who so willingly shared their deepest secrets and experiences with me and also permitted me to share their life stories with the whole world. Thank you so much!! I am also grateful to all the readers, who will take time out to read Baba's stories and His wondrous teachings. Thanks for joining me in this pure, holy journey of love for Baba Sai!

And now, my deepest, purest and most soulful gratitude to my Baba, my Father, my Sai. Thank You, Baba, for choosing me!! 1 am too petty, too small, too inconsequential for a task as glorious and huge as writing a book on You. Thank You for Your love for me and Your faith in me. Every beat of my heart, every breath that I take, every moment of my existence is because of You and for You, My Big Daddy Baba Sai. You are my World!! ☺

Prologue

Baba Sai stepped into my life like a breath of fresh air. His coming marked the birth of 'a new me'. I changed, my world changed and the world around me changed too. Everything else ceased to exist... all that remained was Baba and 1. His divine love was so overpowering, so abundant that I was completely soaked in it. (I still am and I shall continue to be.) © Every new day brought into my life new miracles ant! new stories of Baba. I felt so full of Baba that soon every tiny cell of my being was overflowing with His love and His presence, and so was all of me. I was overwhelmed with a fullness I had never known In-fore. It was beautiful... I was full to the brim with my Baba's love and now this 'fullness' needed an outlet. All I wanted to do was talk about Him, read about Him, sing His praise, serve Him in whatever ways possible, act in accordance with His teachings, or just sit for hours at length and look at Him. But even then, all this taken together did not provide outlet enough for my brewing emotions. So one day I decided to write every story that 1 heard of Baba and praise Him to my heart's content. And this finally proved to be the best and most fruitful vent for my locked-up love and emotions. Whatever I felt, I wrote... whenever I felt like it, I wrote. Every word of my writing was a celebration of my Baba's love. It made rny heart lighter and, soon, I no longer felt that sensation of choking for lack of an orifice. Whenever anyone shared Baba's grace, I put it into words. I knew not day or night. I remember getting up in the middle of dark, stormy nights, sitting next to the open window and while the clouds poured as rain onto nature, my emotions poured as words onto paper.

In it few years, 1 realized, 1 had quite a huge collection of Baba's stories In my hands. My near ones suggested I bring it into a book, so that all it liaba's devotees could guzzle the nectar of His love to their heart's content. But I was very apprehensive, very unsure. So I prayed to my darling Baba for His blessings and also for an indication that He wanted this book — His hook — to come through me. For this, I especially planned a visit to Snirdi and, with many questions to be answered, I met dear Baba. I loved what had been written. My heart knew that they were Baba's words, not mine. But then, I had been writing for the sheer joy of writing, for the love of Baba. Bringing our a book, well, that was the big question mark, as I had never thought of that option.

I reached Shirdi and secured Baba's blessings at the Samadhi Mandir. I prayed to Baba in all earnestness; if He desired that my writings take the form of a book, He must give me a clear indication.

"Tell me, Baba, if You want me to go on writing and give my writings the shape of a book. I will only do so if it is Your wish. Else I am happy just writing and collecting Your stories."

After praying to Baba, still teary eyed and deeply emotional after seeing His blissful form in the Samadhi Mandir, I reached Baba's Dwarkamai to seek His blessings. 1 love the Dwarkamai: every stone, every wall, every breath of air that we breathe in the Dwarkamai is alive with Baba's Soul. A place where Baba lived for sixty long years naturally vibrates with His Divine Presence. I can sit for hours in the Dwarkamai and read the *Shri Sai Satcharita* (Baba's biography, His life & His teachings) untiringly, if I get an opportunity.

On thai day, the Dwarkamai was overcrowded. There was a long queue for *darshati*. I was tost in Baba, as I walked up the steps, towards the hoiy *asan* (seat), on which Baba would sit each day, His left arm resting on the side railing. 1 bowed before Baba's beautiful picture, which now rests on that holy asan and placed my offering of flowers and sweets at His feet. Then, as I closed my eyes in prayer, ! had a beautiful vision of Baba... He was sitting right in front of me, smiling at me and blessing me with His raised right hand. I felt as though I had transitioned in time, back to the Shirdi when Baba was alive. It was like having a *darshan* of Baba in His physical form, after almost a hundred years of His having taken *samadhi.* 1 was in a state of absolute, divine bliss. At that, 1 opened my eyes with a big smile, bowed before Baba's picture and again prayed before Him that I was still awaiting His indication. Saying this, I picked up the consecrated basket of my offerings from Baba's feet and started walking out. As I slowly walked towards the exit, I felt something piercing my finger and hurting my hand, under the basket that I was carrying. Still wondering, I lifted the basket with my left hand... and... voila!! ☺ in my right palm was Baba's blessing — in my right palm was Baba's answer — a golden 'pen', which strangely enough had 'Baba' written on it. ☺ I know not to this day, where it came from. But I look upon it as my most precious belonging, I wanted an indication 'to write the book' and what more could Baba give me than a 'Golden Pen' in His Dwarkamai, that too inscribed with His very own name? So, Baba placed the pen in my hands and I in turn place this book in your hands. Such is His grace, His love... **"You look to me, I look to you".**

I know that Baba's treasury is ever full and overflowing, but we must prove our worth before we seek the wealth of His treasury of abundance. My worth was my love for my Baba... that is my only qualification or asset. I am nothing, no one. But His love places me at tilt' pinnacle of His crown and brings out words that only He writes. I um only the instrument: He writes, He tells His own stories. Only I know the secret that after writing pages and pages, when I stop, I am compelled to refer to the dictionary to check the meaning of words written by my very own hands.... Words that I have never read or known before but strangely enough words that I have appropriately UNt'tl in my book. What bigger proof can 1 give that each word, each Irwm, each teaching comes from Baba and only from Baba? I am like tlii' sunflower that moves in whatever direction tru? sun moves. And li.iba Is my sun... 1 just follow Him, my eyes closed, my heart open. ©

After coming back from Shirdi, my writing happily continued and it took me a few more years to peacefully and patiently complete my book. And then, just a few days before handing over the book to my publishers, I experienced the same anxiousness, the same doubts clouding my mind.... Should I hand over the book for printing or should I just hold it back as my treasured collection? After years, I was once again going through the same emotions. Have I done justice to Baba's book? Will the book be welcomed and loved by the readers? Is Baba happy and satisfied with my efforts?? Deep in thought, praying to Baba for guidance, 1 fell asleep, only to wake up to another divine indication of Baba's wish. 1 dreamt a dream that morning. ☺ In the dream I was in Shirdi with my husband. As he stood near Baba's idol at the Samadhi Mandir and prayed, I stood a little far behind and waited. I couldn't see Baba's idol as the patiiiitfi was standing right in front. So I moved back, now facing the side wall of the Samadhi Mandir. It looked exactly the way it stands today... made of dark greyish stone. Suddenly, 1 saw beams of light on the wall, just like laser beams. I thought someone standing behind me may have turned on a projector. But when I turned, no one was there. And behold!! Before I could understand what was happening, bright colourful beams were playing on the wall, swaying in different directions, as though dancing to a tune. As they slowly merged together — Aum Sai Ram! Right before my eyes was a huge, alive Babaji... smiling, grinning and looking back at me. I screamed aloud in fascination and excitement for the panditji. He came running and bowed ecstatically before Baba's enigmatic, vivacious, brightly coloured form. As we looked on — hold your breath — the beams started moving again and slowly before my eyes... my Baba became my Book.... Yes, the beams that had taken the form of Baba swayed and danced once again on the wall and merged together once again... but this time as my book. Chapter by chapter unfolded, one after the other on the wall and while I cried in joy, pandify celebrated the gift of the book by singing aloud praises of Baba Sai and offering uncountable namaskars at His feet.

Baba answered all my questions, cleared all my doubts and cleansed me of all my negative thoughts. I had slept praying and wondering if I was doing justice to Baba's book. I had slept doubting if I would succeed in bringing Baba's love and teachings in the hands of His devotees. But Baba — my Baba, the kind Baba — solved every query, wiped away every apprehension... **He transformed Himself into the Book. I can't hold back my joy and gratitude. All I wish to share with each of you wonderful souls, who are reading this book, is that... what you hold in your hands at this moment is not a book, it is Baha Himself. Please treasure this book as a gift of Baba's love. He has in the Samadhi Mandir, at Shirdi, manifested Himself as this Book.** So, please value this blessing of Baba, imbibe the lessons therein and place the book in your shrine, just as you place Baba. For me, this book is a continuation of Baba's *Shri Sai Satcharita.* The *Shri Sai Satcharita* was written by Baba through Shri Hemadpant when Baba was in flesh and blood. And this book — *Sai Baba Is Still Alive* — is written by Baba again, but this time through me. He has come back as this book, for us. He alone knows what He wishes... we are just instruments of His love.

But yes, 1 promise you a beautiful journey of love with Baba. As you read along, there will be happy moments, sad moments, ecstatic moments, teary moments, gooseflesh moments and lots more... ☺ I promise to make you weep uncountable tears of love for dear Baba and make you celebrate uncountable smiles of joy with Him too. Your throat may be parched, at times even choked; your heart may palpitate faster than it does... because Baha's marvels, miracles, messages, majesty and magnanimity will weave magic into your lives. Those moments of tears, of divinely choking, of missing heartbeats, of joyous breathlessness in His love are moments of true devotion and such are the moments in which we merge in our Guru in Cosmic Oneness. So dear readers, please gear up... because Baha's book will provide you with not one but many opportunities to intertwine with Him forever.

Always remember these words of Baba and embed them in your soul: **"Anyone who reads My stories shall be on the road to happiness and eternal contentment. Let My stories, My teachings be in every home and may their reading bring solace to the mind of the readers and bring peace and bliss in their lives. Whenever in fear or pain, hold My book close to your heart and chant My name and all your anxieties shall disappear and you shall be engulfed by a** wave of joy and calmness. In the Katyug, reading My stories, hearing My fame and chanting My name shall bestow upon you happiness in life and salvation in death, because reading My stories is as good as being in My company. Let these stories cleanse your negatives and illumine your character. My love shall draw you out from the clutches of disease and even death. So, read My stories day after day, chapter by chapter, and imbibe every learning, every lesson in your heart and live a life of righteousness, goodness and giving. My love shall light up every path you traverse, every darkness you experience and every grey cloud you come across. Have faith in My words. I am forever with you. I live in your heart. Each time you need Me, just call out to Me with love and I shall run to you, My child." ☺

"Believe Me, though I pass away, My bones in My tomb would be speaking, moving and communicating with those, who would surrender themselves whole-heartedly to Me. Do not be anxious that, I would be absent from you. Tou will hear My bones speaking and discussing your welfare. But remember Me always, believe in Me heart and soul and then, you will be most benefited."

— SAI BABA OF SHIRDI

Baba'a Shirdi and Samadhi Mandir

"Whosoever devoutly offers to Me a leaf, a flower, or a fruit or water, of that pure-hearted man, I accept that pious offering."

Baba was never born, Baba never did die.... The soul is not horn, the soul never dies... the soul is eternal... it is beyond the limitations of time and space... and Sai Baba is the purest Soul to have blessed the earth. "When suffering increases, goodness decreases... When unrighteousness (*adharma*) is prevalent and righteousness (*dharma*) fades away... God steps down on the earth to bless the virtuous and transform the vicious." (*BhagwaA Gita: Chapter IV, 7-8.*)

So also, Sai ISaba, Who is verily God Incarnate, stepped down on the holy land of Shirdi in the 19th century.

He was first seen under a neem tree, deep in meditation; a young, fair and extremely good-looking boy of 16. He sat in an asan, motionless, not distracted by heat or cold, winds or storm. The people of Shirdi were awestruck at this astounding sight of such a young sage in an incredibly deep state of trance. His aura was so calm, so serene that it left a deep, enamouring impact on anyone who merely cast a glance at Him. No one knew where He came from, who His parents were or where He was born. This young, handsome lad of 16 stayed in Shirdi for three years and then suddenly disappeared, only to reappear after some time with a marriage party. He was around twenty when He returned. After that He lived in Shirdi for a span of sixty long years and finally took Mahasamadlri in 1918. A rough estimate of His age made by His devotees indicate that He was probably born in AD 1838. When He alighted from the carts on His return with the marriage party, a priest called Bhagat Mhahapati accosted Him with love, "Ya, Said"

(Welcome, Sai). Ever since, He came to be known as Sai and lives in out hearts to this day as Sai Baba of Shirdi.

This enigmatic, charming boy chose as His home an old dilapidated *masjid* (mosque) and rechristened it as the Dwarkamai. The famous Uwarka of Lord Krishna is a place which is open to all castes, all creeds and all religions. Baba must have had a reason when He decided to name His place of residence as Dwarkamai, because it was and still is open equally to the rich and the poor, the diseased and the able-bodied, the religious and the irreligious. People from every caste, culture, country and creed frequent Baba's magic land of Shirdi and return blessed with endless showers of His kindness and grace.

As a young lad, Sai dressed Himself in a dhoti and a long shirt with a turban on His head. He was very fond of flowers and so He planted jai, jui and marigold in the area adjoining the Dwarkamai and tended them with loving care. Thanks to His unceasing efforts, there grew a garden of beautiful flowers on that fortunate land. At that same site today, stands the Samadhi Mandir of Baba, the sacred mansion, where His body was laid to rest.

A few years before Baba's *Mahanamadhi,* a devotee called Bapusaheb Buti, who was a multimillionaire, had a dream in which Baba ordered him to build a *wada* (a place to lodge pilgrims) with a temple at its centre, Baba's most beloved devotee, Madhavrao Deshpande alias Shama, too, had the same dream. Baba's words in both their visions were the same. **"Build a wada with a temple and I shall fulfil the desires of all."** BapuMiheb was a very humble man with enormous wealth. He also had a desire to build a place of residence for himself in Shirdi. Baba's words gave wings to his thoughts. Then, with Baba's due permission, he began the construction of a palatial mansion called Buti Wada. A plan was drawn to make a temple inside the wada and an idol of Lord Krishna was to be placed there. Once, while on His way to Lendi Bagh (park), Baba looked at the wada under construction and said rather prophetically, **"After the wada is complete, we shall use it ourselves. We shall live, move and play there, embrace each**

other and be happy." Each word of dear Baba is impregnated with very deep meaning. No one understood then what Baba meant but, in due course of time, Baba's words acquired the garb of truth.

The construction went on with utmost enthusiasm and energy but when the work was almost complete, Baba suddenly fell seriously ill. This broke Bapusaheb's heart and made him extremely melancholic that his *wada* would never be sanctified by Baba's divine feet. But the kind, merciful Baba, who knew the secret wishes of His devotees, did full justice to Buti's Wada with His last words, "I do not feel weil in the *masjid.* Keep Me in Buti's stone wada." In accordance with Baba's wish, His body was interred in the central place reserved for the shrine. Baba became Murlidhar Shri Krishna and Buti's Wada became the Samadhi Mandir of Sai Baba. To this day — and hereafter to eternity — Baba, true to His words, lives there, moves around and embraces all His children who go to seek His blessings. As prophesied in Bapusaheb's vision, Baba fulfils the heartfelt desires of each and every devotee who visits the Samadhi Mandir. Baba's Soul is ever alive and present there. Devotees have felt His presence in various ways, inconceivable to the mind but conceivable to the devotee's heart.

I myself have had innumerable experiences of Baba's presence in the Samadhi Mandir. It is not as though one can feel Baba's presence only there. He can be felt, sensed and experienced almost tangibly anywhere and everywhere that the pure-hearted devotee wishes to find Him. But the Samadhi Mandir is a magical place. Every wall, every stone is alive with Baba's Soul. His presence can be felt so strong and so powerful in the Samadhi Mandir that one can almost reach out to Him and embrace Him. The wada smells of Baba, the eyes see Him everywhere, the air breathes Him.© Such is the heaven called Shirdi.

I am tempted to share my most beautiful experience of Baba's magical love that bathed my soul in Shirdi. It was a 'pilgrimage of miracles' right frum the very beginning. Six family friends from Dehradun started on a trip to Shirdi by an early morning train and reached New

Delhi by noon on 25 March, 2005. They had to halt their journey for 2-3 hours and then board the Goa Express at 3pm. My parents decided to pack lunch, snacks and sweets for their journey and, accordingly, Dad and I reached the railway station around 1.30pm to meet them and hand over the food.

They were thrilled and ecstatic about their visit but 1 was just the opposite — very low and morose. 1 had been praying to Baba for a long time to call me to Shirdi but nothing was working out. I was keen on starting a new venture and had taken an oath to do so only after seeking His blessings at Shirdi. But each time I made a plan, it fizzled out and further delayed my new venture. **Baba used to say, "Even the leaf of a tree cannot move without My bidding."** Then who was I to make a plan? It was totally in His hands to call me or not.

I sat in a corner at the station, questioning Baba and my love for Him. I so badly wanted to reach Him, but the doors to Shirdi appeared closed to me. While I was still deep in thought, bombarding Baba with one question after the other, one of my friends spoke up, "Why don't you accompany us right now and fulfil your vow?"

At this, 1 grew even more despondent. "Why are you making suggestions that are not feasible? There is only one hour for the train's departure and I have no tickets, no clothes and no arrangements for the visit. It Is not as If 1 have enough time on hand to come along."

As though providentially, we heard an announcement over the station's loudspeaker: "Goa Express, which is scheduled to depart at 3pm has been delayed by three hours and will now depart at 6pm, Inconvenience caused Is deeply regretted."

I jumped at this information. Oh my God!! Is this for real? The train is delayed!! And liifonvenlencc?? Well, thanks a lot for causing the inconvenience!! ☺

Goa Express, which Is known for always being on time, had actually been delayed. Here was my first miracle... I could now think further aboiit visiting my dear Baba at Shirdi.

But it was not meant to be easy. I had on hand another major issue. The train was now to depart around 6pm but I had to fulfil a work commitment. I had a lecture for MBA students from 7-9pm that same evening and five similar sessions over the next two days. I could not send back 40-50 students in each session due to personal reasons. So, here 1 was back to square one. But my heart was still praying earnestly and Baba never puts down any prayer made with a pure heart. Still unsure whether 1 would be able to make it or not, I went ahead and purchased a general ticket (without reservation) for myself. I decided to go back home and coordinate with my office people for some alternative. I called up the lady, Ganesha, who was in charge of the classes and who, by my good fortune, was an ardent devotee of Baba. She immediately took upon herself the task of organizing some other faculty member to take classes on my behalf. Within half an hour I got a call from her that with Baba's grace she could fix up someone else to conduct all four sessions on the forthcoming days but at such a short notice no one was available for the evening session. I had to take the 7-9pm lecture and we had rm option. 1 was heartbroken... when 1 had just started to feel that my dream to visit Shirdi would come true, here I was at a dead end once again.

I was now back home and, to be honest, feeling far worse than I had felt that morning. Feeling sad at not being able to visit Shirdi was still something 1 could deal with but having an option and still not being able to go was killing, to say the least. I was so full... I could have cried endlessly.

"Baba, this can't be happening to me. You can read my heart. It is so full of love for You!! Don't You need my love the way I need Yours?? Please call me, Baba... please."

My eyes were still shut, when my phone rang and shook me out of my prayers. It was a call from the station: it was close to 5pm and there was just an hour for the train to depart. 1 was sure they were calling to check my final programme. I didn't want to refuse them, but I had no option as my evening class was unavoidable.

After thinking for some time, I finally took the call but before I could speak, I heard my friend's excited voice, "I've called to inform you that the train has been delayed further. It will now depart at 9.20pm. Do you think you can make it now?"

I was stoned... choked... spaced-out; my eyes bathed in tears, I sat back in a state of shock and disbelief. Was 1 dreaming or was all this really happening to me? Baba, dear Baba, had finally opened the doors. I packed my bags, left for my lecture, which I wound up a half hour early and before I knew it, I was on my way to Shirdi. ☺ Baba's miracles, one after the other, had opened all the locked doors in my way.

Shirdi to us devotees is always like a dream. The happiness, the bliss and the ecstasy that we experience is beyond the scope of words or language. Each visit has its own charm, its own divinity but little did I know that this unplanned, miraculous visit to Shirdi was yet to unfold the most beautiful moments of ray life.

It all happened on 28th March, a delightful Monday, ft was around 4.30am and we were in Baba's wondrous Samadhi Mandir for the *Kakad Aarti* (Morning Prayer). It was undoubtedly my life's most beautiful morning. 1 had never felt so close to Baba. I felt as if I was in paradise. I could sense Baba as though He was alive and physically present all around me... everywhere. 1 could see Him with my heart... I could hear Him with my soul. Words fail me, when I attempt to describe the fountain of emotions that drenched me to my core. AH I can recall is that I was hysterical and so overpowered by my love for Baba that I just could not hold back my tears. I had brought along with me a bunch of roses, which I wanted to place at Baba's feet. And like every other time, 1 was very cautious, so that not even a petal, let alone a rose, broke off. Holding the bunch, cradled safely in both my hands, I cried my heart out throughout the *aarti* and even after. Baba awakens in us *Soham* (Thou Art That) consciousness. His mere presence burns away the physical body made out of matter and the subtle body created out of conditioned thoughts and karmic payoffs. He awakens in His devotees a feeling of Cosmic Oneness, where the identification with the physical and subtle body melt away, all barriers get shattered and all that remains is a Divine Soulful Oneness. Lost in the Soham state, all that I kept repeating with each breath was, "1 love You, Baba." I looked on at His life-sized idol without batting an eyelid, even though my vision was blurred due to tears. I was not crying because I was in any pain or sorrow, nor was there anything I wished to ask for: the only emotion that made me weep on and on was my overflowing love for my Baba Sai. Like I said before, the air of the Samadhi Mandir is so full of Baba that merely breathing it cleanses us of all negativity, washes away our sins and bad thoughts, and fills us with a feeling of Divine Oneness (*Aitvaita* or Non-Duality).

Once the aarti was over, we all moved forward in a queue towards Baba's life-like idol to seek His blessings. There was a huge rush of devotees and subsequently the management inside the temple got into action. They divided us into two columns so that we would quickly clear out of the temple and make place for other devotees who were awaiting their turn. In the confusion that followed, 1 was pushed away from the rest of my friends, into a separate queue that was moving out very fast. My tears gushed out when 1 realized that I was the only one out of my group who would be out of the. temple in no time, while my friends had managed to stick to the inner queue that was moving very slowly and so they would get to spend a much longer time with Baba before they came out.

"Baba!!" I cried out. "1 reached You with so much difficulty, overcoming so many challenges and I don't even get a peaceful moment with You? I must be a very sinful, bad child. Don't You love me, Baba? But despite everything, I love You, Baba. I really love You."

As I sobbed my way out, holding my bunch of red roses in my hand for Baba and repeating my "I love You" without a pause, a very strange thing happened. A very tall person, robed in the livery of Baba's Uniformed Escorts (*bhaldars*) — those Escorts that stand right in front of Baba's idol in a red traditional dress and chant His praise in a very loud, high-pitched tone at the end of the aarti — walked up to me. He smiled at me, broke away a rose from the bunch in my hand and walked away with it. I was in a state of complete shock and disbelief. I was extremely hurt and upset as 1 couldn't understand why he had behaved in such a bizarre manner. When I tried to question him, all he replied was, "Baba." I really could not understand what he was saying in his native language but, by this time, I was convinced that Baba was upset with me for some reason unknown to me. I was being pushed out without even getting an opportunity to spend time with Him or seek His blessings peacefully and, now, He didn't even want my roses and so someone had just walked up to me and ruined my little bunch of flowers!

As I moved on, still shaken by what had just happened, 1 reached Baba's *samadhi,* just before exiting the temple. "Baba, please say You love me too, before I leave. Else I will be shattered, Baba. Please, Baba; please say '1 love you'." When I was about to bow down at His feet, tearful and distressed, the same man in red clothes walked out of another door. This time he was holding something else in his hand. It was Baba's glorious gold crown. When he saw me looking at him in surprise, he gave me a big smile and pointing towards something, repeated his monosyllable "Baba". What he now pointed at was my life's most unbelievable sight. I had repeated a hundred times by now, "I love You, Baba" and, here, right before my eyes was Baba's response. I had said it with tears and He said it with a red rose. Yes, unbelievable as it may sound, on the pinnacle of Baba's golden crown was my tiny little red rose. And right before my eyes Baba was made to wear His crown. And in the Samadhi Mandir, at Shirdi, Baba sat on His throne looking divine and adorned with a token of my love in the form of my tiny rose. ☺

What more could I have asked for? In fact, what more can any devotee ask for? To understand the joy and bliss that 1 experienced that morning, devotees will have to step into my shoes and feel the gamut of emotions running through me. It was now that I understood why I had got pushed into the fast-moving queue. Had I not been in that particular spot, Baba's Escort would have picked a rose from some other devotee's bunch. He walked out of the office door and i was right in front of him. So he took away a rose from me. And not to forget, this emotional drama was written, directed and produced by none other than our dear Sai Baba! He goes out of His way to reaffirm our faith in His love.

When devotees visit Shirdi, we yearn for our little gifts to reach Baba's feet at the Samadhi Mandir. And my gift of love reached not only His feet but also His crown. I'm told that the rose that adorns Baba's crown each day, comes along with His clothes and garlands and is provided by the Sansthan (Temple Governing Body). Under normal circumstances, it is not taken from the devotees. But on that delightful day He accepted my love in the form of the rose and told me in His unique way, "I love you, too." ☺

Just seeing Baba's effulgent form in the Samadhi Mandir destroys all our sins. Shedding tears of love cleanses the impact of all negative sainskaras and karmas. Merely being in His presence imparts the wisdom drawn from all the scriptures of the world. And then when the eyes meet and the soul connects, there is love, there is joy and there are divine miraculous experiences of Oneness. So, cherish and live to the fullest, every moment of joy spent in the Samadhi Mandir. See Him, feel Him, breathe Him and love Him, for there is no feeling more blissful, no place more sacrosanct than Baba's Samadhi Mandir.

Aum Sai Shri Sal Jaya Jaya Sai

"If a man utters My name with love, 1 shall fulfil all his wishes, increase his devotion. And if he sings earnestly My life and My deeds, him I shall beset in front and back and on all sides. Those devotees, who are attached to Me, heart and soul, will naturally feel happiness, when they hear these stories. Relieve Me that if anybody sings My Lcelas, / will give him infinite joy and everlasting contentment. It is My special characteristic to free any person, who surrenders completely to Me, and who does worship Me faithfully, and who remembers Me, and meditates on Me constantly. How can they be conscious of worldly objects and sensations, who utter My name, who worship Me, who think of My stories and My life and who thus always remember Me? I shall draw out My devotees from the jaws of Death. If My stories are listened to, all the diseases will hcyot rid of. So, hear My stories with respect; and think and meditate on them, assimilate them. This is the way of happiness and contentment. The pride and tyjaism of My devotees will vanish, the mind iiflhi- heawrx will be set at rest; and if it has wholchftirifii and complete faith, it will be one with Supreme (`.onsciousncss. The simple remembrance of My name «j '&»', Sai' will do away with sins of speech and hearing."

— SAI BABA OF SHIRDI

Baba's Stories as Divatyas

"If My Leelas are written, the Avidya will vanish and if they are attentively and devoutly listened to, the consciousness of the worldly existence will abate and strong waves of devotion and love will rise up. If one dives deep into My Leelas, he would get precious jewels of knowledge."

We are truly blessed to be born in this era of 'spiritual rising' and 'ascension'. And we are even more blessed because in this era no formal, ritualistic worship is expected of us. All that is expected is thinking of the Lord, remembering Him silently in the heart and chanting His Holy name. But unfortunately, our mind is instated with the tendency to look outwards and not inwards. We are more inclined towards sense objects and worldly pleasures than towards our inner core and our spiritual self. But Baba's method of overcoming this problem was very simple and highly practical. He said that your mind 'thinks' those thoughts that you choose to give it to think. If you give your mind sensual pleasures, temporal gains and mundane matters to think about, it will cio so. However, if you give it pure thoughts, inner growth and Guru's grace to think of, it will do that too. What your mint! thinks is an initiation made by you and you alone. The more you give it positive thoughts and intellectual .stimulation, the better it is for you.

But in today's busy life, how does one sit back and think of God? We all love Baba but how much time can we spare and, most importantly, with how much concentration can we take His name? To this, Baba gave a pragmatic solution, **"If you can't meditate or concentrate for too long, just sit and read My stories and My teachings. The time and the attention that you give to My stories is equivalent to being in My presence and My company and chanting My name. So, just remember Me and you shall be on the path to joy, success and salvation. Leave of all cleverness and always remember 'Sal', 'Sai'. Anyone who does that would be set free from all shackles and**

bondages and shall get the best of both the worlds."

So, reading Baba's storks, singing His praise and loving Him ardently are the purest methods of reverence and remembrance. Shri Hemadpant has also written in Baba's biography, *Shri Sal Satcharita*:

"The description of Half's pure fame, and the hearing of the same, with love, will destroy (he sins of the devotee. Therefore, this is the simple *sadhana* for attaining joy and salvation. The *sadttana* for Krita Yuga was tranquillity of mind and body, for *Treta Yuga* — Sacrifice, for *Dwapara Yuga* — Worship, and tor Kali (present! Age, it is singing of the name and the glory of the Lord. The other *sadhanas* are very difficult to practise, but **singing and hearing I lie stories and the glory of the Lord (Sal Halm) Is very easy und will give peace and happiness to the people, who are afflicted with sorrows and heavily loaded with miseries of this worldly existence. It will also bestow upon them, knowledge and wisdom, both in the worldly and spiritual domains. It these teachings of Sai Baba, which are as interesting and instructive as the Vedic lore, are listened to and meditated upon, the devotee will get all that they long for."**

Now the path was clear .uul simple. Heading about Baba has always been my most favourite 'Hung lo do'. Hut why not write more and more of His *leelas* anil sing Mis praise SO that millions of others could be benefitted by it too. What could be better than making a collection of His beautiful stories and His divine teachings? Baba's grace shone upon me and I decided that this would be my best and purest offering at Mis feet, I have experienced many delightful events of Baba's grace in my life and In the lives of those around me. And my joy, my love and my elation sparked a million lamps of His Light in every pore of my existence. These lamps illumined my life, changed the way I perceived the world, filled the emptiness within me, making me a happy, peaceful and better human being. My spiritual fullness — 'Baba fullness' as I call It — Inspired this book. Baba gave me infinite indications and blessed me through dreams, prayers and conversations, encouraging me to write and share His *leelas* and His love. The beats of my heart dance to Baba's tune each time I hear or experience His grace and then all these mellifluous vibrations come together as stories of strength and power.

The truth is that I was so complete, so abundant inside, so incredibly topped right up to the brim with Baba's boundless love... that I desperately needed an outlet. If you keep pouring into a vessel, it has to finally overflow. Same was the case with me. Baba was, at every known moment, filling me up with His presence and reaching out to me with His never-ending love. I had no option but to share. And that is how this book happened... yes, it was never planned, Baba kept pouring into me and I kept pouring onto sheets of paper. Before I even realized, I had this book — this precious treasure grove of knowledge and wisdom — in my hands. The world thinks I have written a book... but only I know the truth. I am too petty and Inconsequential for a task so enormous, so vast. **Baba used me as Instrument of His love to create this book for His children. My hands did move but the words were Baba's. He smiled and my pen smiled; He narrated and my hand typed: He cried and I soaked the paper; He blessed and the book reached your hands. This book is, therefor, authored by Baba Himself.** I am not even close to the speck of dust that once touched His feet. Then how could I write about the Lord God Himself? So, the credit and acclaim for writing this work must go to my Baba and Baba alone. His stories and teachings are like divatyas.. inextinguishable candles that light up our lives and out path.

In my years of knowing Baba, I have experienced so many miracles of His love and kindness in my life and in the lives of those around me as well. We do call them miracles for the lack of a better word in language lo describe them. But the more f understood Baba, the more Inappropriate I found this word to be. I realized that the term 'miracle' Is truly hollow and very inapt in expressing Baba's blessings. What we term as 'miracles' are not mere miracles but are deep, fulfilling experiences... they are reaffinnations that Baba is alive in our lives even today. Every time a devotee has called out with love, there has been a response. Baba's heart is soft as wax. He can't see His children in pain. And each time we call out His name with love, He rushes to help us, in the most astounding, unbelievable and inconceivable ways... and we call His love, kindness and care 'Miracles'. ☺

In fact my 'meeting' Baba was in itself a 'miracle', woven around my life by His love. I use the word 'meeting' though I never met Sai Babaji in His human form. Yet 1 have experienced every emotion, every smile, every teardrop and every blessing that I would have experienced had He been alive. Because with Babaji it just doesn't matter that He left His body almost a hundred years back; He is still alive in every possible, conceivable manner. I can see Him, feel Him, talk to Him, smile at Him and see Him smile hack at me. He holds my hand and leads me on... every moment, every day. And on days that are tough, paths that are laden with thorns, He carries me in His Holy Arms and wipes away all my fears. He is my strength, He is my wisdom, He is my soul, He is my all. And trust me, not just me but every devotee of Babaji would have experienced this bliss, this joy and this presence in their lives.

I experienced this divinity rather late, after having lived 29 almost-empty years of my life. It was a bright Sunday morning but I was at my darkest worst. Life was just not going the way I would have wanted it to. There were troubles and problems galore. And since I did not yet know dear Baba, I lacked the courage and the conviction to face the odds or stay calm in the midst of the tempest. I would normally sit at home with my family on such low days and feel much better in their loving company but this day was different. Burdened with the load of a hundred worries, I woke up, bathed, dressed, walked out of my house, sat in my car and started driving blindly... with nowhere to go, no destination to reach. I kept driving from one road to another, one lime to the other, aimless, directionless and probably even mindless. On my gloomy days, if I was not with my family, one could trace me to a temple, a *gurudwara* or a *dargah*. But this one day, 1 didn't want to go to any such place that would be crowded. 1 wanted to be alone, and .ill hy myself. I was still driving purposelessly, when i saw this huge, white-coloured, brand-new building straight ahead. I don't know why, but I stopped my car. 1 promise you, I had no idea what the place was.

It appeared like a shrine or a temple. The strange thing is I had just decided that I did not want to visit a temple, but I inadvertently stopped at a place which appeared like one.

I parked my car, took off my shoes at the stand outside and walked in. I climbed up the stairs of the building, wondering where I was headed, little knowing that my entire life was going to change, that my world was going to go topsy-turvy, that magic was about to begin. ©

I looked up, right in front... *and our eyes met.* I froze, I swear I did. And suddenly my vision got blurred... what was this in my eyes... tears?? And tears they were, i knew not why I wept but 1 wept like crazy. There was no reason but it was as though I had been overpowered by a flood of tears. Just as I stepped in closer, 1 heard the sound of the conch, followed by the ringing of bells. 1 realized that the prayer service (aarti) had commenced. 1 observed a number of devotees around me clapping and singing along with the main priest, accompanied by the sound of drums and several other musical instruments. But this observation was fleeting. As my gaze went back to those divine eyes, the tears came back yet again. And I cried aloud for the rest of the half hour while the prayer ceremony went on, my face concealed by my long hair to avoid catching the attention of the devotees around me. 1 don't recall weeping like this ever before in my life.

As I sat down at the end of this prayer session and closed my eyes, I had something like a flashback. I knew these eyes, but how?? Who is this fiod'n He looks familiar.... And then I remembered. 1 recalled a very tiny picture of this God in our temple at home. 1 knew those eyes.., in tact, it felt as if I had known them through several lifetimes; I could feel a deep connection. And then I went back to the last few days of my messed-up life. Each time I would step into the temple room in our house, I would fight with the deities in there (I mean their pictures obviously). I was going through a very rough phase and 1 would tussle with them to make things better, "Can't You feel my pain?? Why are You deaf to my prayers??" I would persist. And then over the last week or may be ten days, my eyes had intermingled with 'these' familiar eyes. I hadn't — and still haven't — come across more caring, loving and affectionate eyes as these. They had held my gaze and pierced my soul and now 1 clearly remembered speaking to the elderly face in the picture in my temple at home, "Why don't You intercede for me?7 No one is paying heed to my prayers. Your eyes look so full of love... if this love is true then You come to my rescue... why are You sitting In the temple and smiling while 1 am dying of pain?? Do something If You are really God!"

And to my utter disbelief, the old man's eyes had made me drive blindly (without using mine) and led me straight to His own temple, which 1 did not even know existed, till half an hour back. I had walked up the steps of this temple, agonized by turmoil, pain and disillusionment. And here 1 was, exactly half an hour later, in a state of peace and bliss that I had not known in the last 29 years of my existence, experiencing an emotion I had never known or felt before. I could see, feel or hear nothing... my eyes were captivated by His eyes, and my heart entwined with His gracious, blissful smile. He was none other than **Sai Baba of Shirdi.**

The day, 10 March, 2002, Sunday, has been etched deep in my memory. It has now been ten long years and today after about 3,650 days, as I sit down to pen my experience, I realize the inadequacy and limitation of words to express my subliminal feelings and emotions. My tears are still as fresh as they felt ten years back, my hands feel Incapable of keying in my tumultuous thoughts and my heart is heating an extra beat every second. Falling in love can be so beautiful, so fulfilling: Baba's love made me realize this. I am still in love with Him, but now it is far, far deeper and divine. My life has changed; my world has changed. 1'ain no longer has the slightest dispiriting impact on rne and joy no longer elates me beyond a certain comfortable level. 1 live in bliss, in calmness... 1 have since then lived a halcyon existence; I can't put it into the words of man-made language, suffocated by syntaxes and rules. But if I do attempt, all 1 can say is... my soul has been touched, cleansed and awakened and has fallen in love. A love that goes beyond those bright, deep eyes... and connects with the Soul of my Gum, my God... Sai Baba. Just looking at Him dissolves the feeling of duality between Him and me. I feel a vibrant Oneness. **His blessings are my treasure, His love my wealth. His grace my joy and His presence my breath.** I love reading — have always loved it — but my true education has been during my meditation on Baba, in which 1 have travelled far and wide, over the mountains, beyond the seven seas and right up into space. I have seen the unseen, felt the unknown and touched the non-tactile. We have floated into tipples of love, oceans of light. We have dived into divine waters. It has been strange... the deeper we have dived together, the higher has my soul risen. My learning, my knowledge and my innate wisdom have blossomed in long conversations that I have had with Him. He is the Love of my Life, my Best Friend, my Guide, my Father... my Big Daddy, as 1 lovingly address Him. He is my Sai Baba.

Aum Sai Shri Sai Jaya]aya Sai

"Do not try to yet mantra or upadesh [instructions] from anybody. Make Me the sole object of your thoughts and actions; and you will, no doubt, attain paramartha [the spiritual goal of life]. Look at Me wholeheartedly, and I, in turn, look at you. Sitting in this Masjid, I speak the truth, nothing but the truth. No Sadhanas or proficiency in the six Shastras is necessary. Have faith and confidence in your Guru. Believe that Guru is the sole Actor or Doer. Blessed is he who knows the greatness of his Guru and thinks him to be Hari, tiara and Brahma (Trimurti,) Incarnate."

— SAI BABA OF SHIRDI

Baba's Twin favourites: Shraddha and Saburi

"I resorted to My Guru for 12 years. He brought Me up. There was no dearth of food and clothing. He was full of love or say, he was love incarnate. How can I describe it? He loved Me most. Rare is a Guru like him. When I looked at him, he seemed as if he was in deep meditation, and then we both were filled with Bliss. Night and day, I gazed at him with no thought of hunger and thirst. Without him, I felt restless. I had no other object to meditate, nor any other thing than My Guru to attend. He was My sole refuge. My mind was always fixed on him. This Nishtha (Faith) is one pice of Dakshina, that I gave to My Guru. Saburi (Patience or Perseverance) is the other pice, I waited patiently and served My Guru. This Saburi will ferry you across the sea of this mundane existence. Saburi removes all sins and afflictions, gets rid of calamities in various ways, and casts aside all fear, and ultimately gives you success. Saburi is the mine of virtues, consort of good thought. Nishtha *(Faith) and Saburi (Patience) are like twin sisters, loving each other very intimately."*

In return for His love, all Baba wanted from His children were the twin virtues of faith and patience: Shraiiilha and Sahuri. **Firm faith and perseverance, combined with devotion and love for the Lord, are the quintessential virtues of a human being.** Faith and confidence in Baba's loving feet free us from all afflictions. And patience, the most superior of virtues, when combined witli faith, blesses us with material benefits and enriches us spiritually as well. But all qualities are incomplete without love, which i.s .symbolic of God Himself, **Love is the soul of prayer, the driving force behind faith and the spirit of patience.** Without love no prayer is complete, nor can cords of oneness with the Lord be tied in an eternal unbreakable knot.

Faith should never be blind. Experiment on your belief and the positive results will convert your belief into strong faith. **Belief put into successful experiment is faith.** I had deep, immense belief and conviction that Baba would run to me in my hour of distress and He always did — and today my faith stands firm and unshaken, even in the most turbulent times. Faith cannot be put to comparison or weighed on .1 scale. There is nothing such as little faith or less faith. We sometimes say, "I have faith that God will help me solve my problem but why is it taking so long?" This is a question that contradicts itself. Where there are 'Ifs' and 'huts', there can be no faith. The moment the word 'but' comes in our prayers, the prayer loses its value. Either there is complete faith or there's no faith. So trust Baba and believe in your heart that it may take time hut Baba will do the 'best' He can. **Faith must be consummate, beyond comparison and not limiting on itself.**

Another important lesson to remember is that an act of waiting peacefully because of lack of alternatives cannot be construed as patience. **Patience is a self-imposed act of inner strength and hope, a result of one's surrender to His divine predisposition.** True patience reaps a rich harvest, both material as well as spiritual.

Innumerable events during Baba's lifetime proved again and again that if a devotee was resolute in his faith, waiting with complete, undeterred patience for Baba's love to shine upon him... it always did shine. Incurable diseases were cured, those dying got a fresh lease of life, and Ihose that were shattered got their strength renewed... the list is countless. And even today, when Baba is not present in the body, the miracles of the twin virtues continue unabated. **The S*hri Sai Satcharita* says, "As a devotee is resolute and determined, so is Baba's Immediate response. Sometimes Baba puts the devotees to severe lest; and then gives them *'Upadesh'* [instructions]."** So let us not get deluded by the tests or their duration and hold our ground firm.

Yet, there are times when our faith is strong but our prayers go unanswered — don't lose faith as Baba knows what is best for us.

If one door does not open, then may be another door is yet to open... and He has something better in store for us. Surrender completely to your Guru, your Baba. Let there be no doubts, no questions, no complaints. Learn to have complete faith in Him. If you can do this, your problems will either cease to exist or become very insignificant. **Whenever you are confronted by a difficult situation or a problem that you cannot solve, give it to Baba.** He is our Sai Maa and who would worry more about the child than the Maa, the Universal Mother? When you do surrender your problems and yourself at His feet, stop thinking or worrying. Just be an onlooker and watch smilingly how Baba unties the knots and answers ali the questions that once troubled your heart. If you can adopt this, your life will become glorious with the grace of the kind Baba.

Now, to add shine to your gold, heat it in fire. Yes, to Strengthen your faith in Baba, add to it a lot of patience. Baba always said that 'patience' (Saburi) is the topmost virtue in a human being. So, **when our faith (Shraddha) comes with a topping of Saburi, it signifies the stage of complete surrender.** Baba will be very pleased and will accept you most willingly at His feet.

Always remember that the life we are living today is a mirror of our past karmas. What you have done in the past will be reflected by this mirror in our present, and our actions today will decide the future course of our life. Let faith and perseverance in His Holy Feet give us the courage and the inner strength to live a good present, despite all adversities. And let today's virtues and good actions carve out the path for our fulfilling and bright future. The remembrance of Baba's name will take us across the ocean of maya (illusion) and the practice of virtues such as charity and love will enrol us as permanent members in Baba's durbar (court). So give yourself unto Him, surrender yourself at His feet and let Him take complete control of your lives; because the truth remains that 'our life is ultimately in Baba's benevolent hands'.

I have come across such moving experiences of 'faith' and 'patience' that my heart skips a beat at their mere thoughl. I must share with you that the impossible becomes possible, the loss becomes a gain and death comes back to life... when the devotee does not give in to life's challenges and clings to Baba with *Shaddha* and *Saburi*.

Let me share my meeting with an elderly gentleman called Narayan* (whom 1 address as Uncle Narayan) near Baba's Gurusthan, on a visit to Shirdi. He appeared to me, in our first meeting, like a bee addicted to the nectar of the world's most beautiful flower called Sai. I could see fascination, endearment and affection for Baba in his eyes, as he narrated the most painful — yet the most memorable — moment of his life... which became my greatest lesson of undiluted faith and perseverance.

This incident took place in 1995. His son Sai (see his obsessive love for Baba that he had even named his son Sai), who was studying in a reputed college in Mumbai, was to represent his institution in an inter-college cricket match. He was excellent at sports and his college had very high expectations from him. The match was going on really well, and students and family were busy cheering the respective teams, when Sai suddenly left the field. He asked for medical help as he was kvllng nauseous and sick. But before much could be done, he started vomiting. The doctor was consulted and he said that there was nothing lo worry, as it appeared to be heat stroke. Sai was given light medication and advised to take a little rest.

Over a week went by but Sai's vomiting did not abate. In fact, his health only grew worse and the vomiting too increased in frequency each day. There was not the slightest improvement in his condition. His family was obviously very concerned and they consulted the doctor once again, who advised a few tests. The reports indicated a problem and Sai was diagnosed with chronic jaundice.

Uncle Narayan told me that in Mumbai several home remedies are available for jaundice. So they tried several treatments, including the

*Name changed to protect identity

one recommended by the doctor. However, instead of improving, Sai's condition deteriorated each day. He then went through a sonography and a severe malignant infection was detected in his stomach. The doctors could not figure out the cause behind the infection. The jaundice further worsened; Sai's condition grew from bad to worse. Several doctors were consulted but nothing helped.

Uncle told me, "He was withering before my eyes and I could do nothing. Doctors too appeared to be slowly giving up as they did not know what line of treatment to try next. Nothing, just nothing was helping. We were losing all hope of Sai's recovery but our faith on dear Baba did not falter even a wee bit." So, the family was helpless but continued praying, as Sai did not respond to any medicine or any treatment.

The family members took turns to sit beside him and prayed with all their faith- One night, Uncle Natayan compelled Aunty (his wife) to get some sleep, while he sat beside his ailing son, looking over him. "A few hours went by. I was praying next to Sai when he slowly opened his tired eyes and looked at me very affectionately. I smiled back and a prayer exploded out of my grieving heart that my Sai should keep smiling like this all his life."

But alas! This was not to be. Sai suddenly looked uneasy and looked at his father helplessly as if trying to say something; his breathing became very heavy and then suddenly he collapsed... mouth open, tongue sticking out, unconscious and lifeless. Uncle cried aloud and could make out from Sai's closed eyes and protruding tongue that something was seriously wrong. His heart palpitated in distress, 'Is this the end?' Low pulse... he screamed for help. Family members rushed to the room. They frantically tried to revive Sai; someone checking his heartbeat, some his pulse and some his breathing. But then time seemed to stop and so also Sai's heartbeats. They were still contemplating either calling in a doctor or rushing him to the hospital, though they knew in their hearts that it may not help.

But... right before all this noise and commotion, Sai's mother lay asleep in the other room, oblivious to the impending storm. She had been weeping day and night for the past several days but had not given up hope because she knew that even if all doctors had given up on any chances of Sai's recovery, her father, her Baba — the doctor of doctors — would never deny her help. That night too, she lay weeping and praying and fell into deep sleep. And then as if to answer her prayers, Baba walked towards her, in her dream, looking magnificent in His august presence. As she sat crying for her baby's recovery to good health, Baba, dear Baba, placed His gracious hand on her head and smiled, "Chinta kyu kar rahi ho? Diya bitjhne wala tha par mem use kyu Imjtwe dunga? Woh theek ho jayega... subati." ("Why are you worrying? The lamp was flickering and was about to get extinguished but why will I let it die down? He will be fine... in the morning.")

At this, Aunty jumped awake to the sound of loud cries in the house and ran to her son's room.

"He's gone," cried Uncle Narayan. "Our son has gone forever."

Aunty stood still. Her eyes were seeing something that her heart was refusing to believe. She ran to Uncle, the dream still very fresh in her mind

"No, this cannot be true. My Sai cannot leave me and go. Nothing will happen to him. He will be fine by morning."

Uncle told me at Baba's Gumsthan, "I looked at her and cried even londei, I thought she was hysterical and was in too much pain to believe what her eyes were seeing. She couldn't bear the loss of her young son. I tried to console her, but she forced me to be quiet and narrated her dream to me, crying despairingly at the same time. Initially 1 was blank. I did not know how to react to her dream. 1 had |ust lost my only son, in all intelligence l knew he was no more and here was my wife, insisting that he would be fine by the morning," at this Uncle paused

.

Then his gaze moved far way into space, as he continued, "I spent a lew minutes in calming my nerves. I loved Baba too much to not trust His words. He would never come in a dream if He did not wish well. Baba's walking up to my wife at the same time when Sai was collapsing and telling her with love that he would be fine, could never be wrong... so, both of us, decided with unwavering faith, to wait patiently till the morning. Despite the many arguments put up by other family members, we sat near Sai's lifeless body and prayed, wept and chanted all night. We didn't tali a doctor nor did we rush to a hospital; we just waited. It seemed like ages. The night was so long."

A new day dawned, awaiting new magic. The first rays of the sun lit up the dark skies. As if disturbed by the bright light, the eyebrows moved and then slowly the eyes opened. Yes, my friends... they were the eyes of young Sai.

"Good morning," he said, as he smiled at his mother and father. "1 am feeling much better today."

Uncle and Aunty hugged him and wept like mad. Sai had no idea why, for he did not know that Baba had drawn him back from the cruel jaws of death. His health improved day by day and all reports came normal. Soon he was back in college with no signs of any ailment. He was — and still is — healthy and happy.

I have heard many leelas of dear Baba, I have seen the most unbelievable miracles but this blessing was unique. He brought His child back from the door of death or should I say from death itself. Words fail me today; how can silly, stupid me describe His greatness? Where would I find the words? All I can say is that **Baba's love call change the course of our destiny. His loving eyes can put life back into the dead; for He is the Lord God: our Creator, our Preserver, but I am sure not the Destroyer. He is our Father, our**

Mother, our God Sai. Anyone who has firm faith backed up by patience and love can experience Baba's grace and overwhelming miracles, every single day, every single moment of life. For... the twin sisters of Shradciha and Saburi are the greatest saviours, the worthiest virtues.

Aunt Sai Shri Sai Jaya Jaya Sai

"He who loves Me most, always sees Me. The whole world is desolate to him without Me, he tells no stories but Mine. He ceaselessly meditates upon Me and always chants My name. I feel indebted to him who surrenders himself completely to Me a-nd ever remembers Me. I shall repay his debt by giving him salvation

(self-realization). I am dependent on him who thinks and hungers after Me and who does not eat anything without first offering it to Me. He who thus comes to Me, becomes one with Me, just as a river gets to the sea and becomes merged (one) with it. So leaving out pride and egoism and with no trace of them, you should surrender yourself to Me Who am seated in your heart."

— SAI BABAOFSHIRDI

Hungry for Food Cooked with Love

"Those who are fortunate and whose demerits have vanished, take to My warship. If you always say 'Sai, Sai', I shall take you over the seven seas; believe in these words, and you will he certainly benefited. I do not need any paraphernalia of worship. I rest there where there is full devotion."

This little story dates back to the time when Baba was living in Shirdi. One day, as Shri Hemadpant and some other devotees sat at Baba's feet, a few grams (chana) rolled down Hemadpant's sleeves. Everyone in the proximity who observed this started smiling.

Then Baba said affectionately, "Why were you eating the grams alone, without sharing them with those around? See, now you are caught."

At this Hemadpant replied, "Baba, 1 never eat alone and always share with those present next to me. Then why do you shoulder this bad habit on me?"

Baba smiled, "1 know you share everything you eat, with those around you, but when you are alone... do you share with Me? Am T not always with you?"

These words of Baba are priceless. Those who understand the depth of these words will never again take a single bite of food or a single sip of water without first offering it to dear Baha. We know that He is always with us, within us. So when we eat, how can we eat alone? It is criminal to satiaie our hunger but keep our Baba starving. **We must always take His name and serve Him before partaking of any**

food or drink. If there is no idol or picture of Baba nearby, then we must close our eyes, visualize Him and make the offering. But never ever should we eat alone... because we are never alone. He Is always with us.

Baba taught a life-changing lesson by His words. Through His simple language and unassuming ways, He showed us how to rid ourselves of our vices and negatives. **The lesson is that not only food but all our sensory pleasures should be laid at Baba's feet. Before we enjoy any worldly objects, we must first take His name or remember Him.** This is equivalent to making an offering to Him. By doing this, we can control our bad habits and immoralities. **If we think of Baba before every action, we will never act in a manner to cause harm or hurt. If we think of Baba before every meal, we will never partake of forbidden or harmful food or drinks. If we think of Baba before enjoying sensual or worldly pleasures, we will never indulge in immoral practises.** So all in all, we will be better human beings, far more upright and noble. Because when we offer unto Baba something that we know is evil or unacceptable, we will certainly feel abashed and humiliated before Him. And this is reason enough for us, His children, to transform ourselves and be able to look straight into His eyes with love and not with eyes lowered in embarrassment.

Baba loves it when we cook for Him and feed Him with motherly affection. He craves for our attention and our care just as we do for His. He has an exclusive room in His heart and a special place in heaven for those devotees who always offer Him food before eating. He accepts their devotion most willingly and grants them bliss supreme.

Baba's Shirdi is always welcoming, brimming with sweet memories and enchanting experiences. Every visit to Shirdi further strengthens our faith in His Divine Presence and gives our heart a hundred new reasons to rejoice. From the moment we step down on the Holy Land, till we leave... it is pure happiness. Feels like heaven. 1 don't know what heaven is like; I mean after dying those who go to heaven, well, 1 haven't shared their experiences so far. © But 1 can surely share mine, as I keep re-visiting the Heaven of Shirdi again and again — it is just never, ever enough. The same happened, yet again, on my visit to Shirdi (in 2007) when I met I.alita, a very graceful and charming lady. Of my many experiences of joy, let me share a special one. We met at the Dwarkamai and there she narrated her life's most beautiful experience to me. How and why we met, I'll explain a little later. But her story was a true eye-opener, an example of pure devotion, faith and patience.

She was a lovely woman, who had spent her entire life at Shirdi. We would consider her immensely fortunate, as she was one of the blessed few who were born and brought up in Baba's homeland. But Lalita would have disagreed with me — had 1 met her nine months back — because despite having lived in Shirdi, life had been very unfair to her and her family (so she told me). Her husband did not have a job and used to make a living by selling packets of lobaan (incense granules) outside the Dwarkamai. These were the times when even ?100 had no value due to excessive inflation and his only means of livelihood was selling packets of lobaan worth ?2 each. Readers can well imagine their plight, a family of six: Lalita, her husband, their two daughters and two sons surviving on practically nothing. There was no money, no work. Each day was a challenge and each night a struggle.

Lalita told me that they had been quite well-off earlier and had lived a comfortable life. She had never even felt the need to take up a job, as her husband earned enough to support the family. But after he lost his job, they were plagued, overwhelmed by difficult times;,today, he was as good as jobless and she was ready to do just about anything to feed her children. She was an intelligent, capable and elegant woman, as was very clear even during my first meeting with her. She could have easily got a decent job but when times are bad, things just don't fall in place and that is exactly what happened with her. Even after several wholehearted attempts, she could get no work. Disheartened, yet desperate, she took up the job of washing utensils in one of the below-average restaurants at Shirdi. She was shattered.

In her words, "I hated it! 1 used to cry every day and forced myself to wash the utensils. I was helpless. I had to do it. We could not have survived without food for much longer."

She told rne that the days spent at this job were the most depressing and painful days of her life. If you tell a woman from a reasonably well-to-do family to wash the dishes of hundreds of people with her own hands — hands that have possibly not even washed her own dishes — it had to be awful. (As in India, even people from reasonably well-off families are accustomed to hiring maids to do the dishes.)

Baba always said, "Why fear, when 1 am there??" And true to His words, He was, is and will remain to eternity the life-force, the inner-Strength, and the ever-burning lamp in each of His devotee's hearts. His eyes, spilling over with love and kindness, give us the courage to move on and the will to survive, despite every test and every failure. With broken hearts, traumatized minds and darkened shadows all around us... our faith stands strong, unfazed and irrepressible. Nothing can shatter or even slightly shake a devotee's true faith in Baba's feet. Similar was the case with Lalita. She had been subjected to poverty, pain and suffering and had spent innumerable sleepless nights and days when she had gone without food. But all these negative forces iaken together, however big they may have appeared, could not even touch Lalita's faith in her Father, Sai Baba.

It had been four continuous years, without a break or even a day's gap, that she had attended Baba's Kakact Aitrii (Morning Prayer). And as easy as it may sound, it is just not easily doable. I recall a time some years ago, when 1 had taken an oath before Baba and visited His temple, in Delhi, each morning for the same Morning Prayer, 11 days in a row. And I can tell by personal experience that it took a lot of willpower to wake up at 3.30am each day, bathe in the freezing cold (as it was the winter season), dress up and drive to the temple before 4.3()am. To do the same at Shirdi was far more difficult as there are a

large number of people waiting to enter the main tempk for the prayer. At times, one has to get in the queue as early as midnight to be able to get inside the temple before the prayer.
So Lalita would wake up at odd hours each morning, bathe and reach Baba's Dwarkamai at the earliest possible, in order to attend the Kakad Atirti. Day after day, undaunted by summer or winter, she was there morning after morning to wake up her father and seek His blessings. This was not all. After attending the Morning Prayer, Lalita would go home and cook whatever little she could manage to and bring it back to feed Baba at the Dwarkamai. For those of yon who are not aware, let me mention that Baba left His body in 3918. When I write that devotees wake Him up or feed Him, I am referring to His lift-sized idol and His pictures. His physical form may not be there anymore but for each devotee He is still alive and breathing. After going home and doing her puja (saying her prayers), she would finally eat something. I salute the lady for such perseverance. It takes immense courage, determination and willpower to follow such a strict regimen for four long years, not to forget the constant struggle to survive without pecuniary means. She is to me a stiining example of Shraiidha and Saburi and truly exemplifies flaba's teachings of faith and patience.

Four years is a long time. In spite of her persistent worship, her prayers were not bearing fruit. At this 1 am reminded of Baba's teaching as to how most human beings give up rather quickly in life, In Baba's words, "Imagine the mango tree in full blossom... a gush of wind and most flowers fall off before bearing fruits." Similarly, we are tested and most of us fall away deluded by the testing winds. '1 hose that stay on bear sweet fruit... reach Him, attain the goal of life. Lallta had faced not only storms and winds but much more; yet her faith remained strong and she firmly held on to Baba's feet with unyielding patience. She was not one of those to fall off from the tree because of turbulent winds.

It was now seven days since she had been washing utensils at the restaurant. She was in unbearable pain. She went to Baba, as usual, for the morning aarti but this morning was very different. For the first time, she broke down completely before Baba and cried her heart out. She was inconsolable.

In her words, "I did not have the strength to go through more suffering. My children were without food, my husband without a job. I begged Raba to come to our rescue."

She was in tears as she took me through that painful day of her life. "Give me some respectable work, Baba. Please give me some work so that we can tide over these difficult times. Please, Baba. I will work with my heart and soul. Rut please show me the way. You are my Father, if you don't help your daughter, who will, Baba? Who will?" So she sobbed at His feet unrelentingly. "Come, Baba, please come and help me get some work."

So He came... would He ever break His daughter's heart? I smile at my Baba's love and His soft-as-a-feather heart. He can bear the burden of the Universe on His strong and mighty shoulders. But He can't bear the burden of our water-light tears. ©

"Don't cry, my child!" said an unfamiliar voice.

Lalita looked up. Bright eyes looked back at her. Clad in a white robe, an elderly person with long white hair and a beard smiled, "Do you want some work?"

Lalita looked up in astonishment; she was still weeping. She thought, "How does he know what I'm thinking in my mind?"

He repeated, "Do you want to do some work?"

"Yes," she responded through tears.

"All right," continued the old man, "take this ?50 and cook something for the Khog Prasad (offering made to God and then distributed as prasad to devotees) at Dwarkamai,"

"I was so lost, so surprised and confused. I was blank and totally brain-tired due to the stress and hours of crying. So, without putting much thought to it, 1 took the money from the old man and went back home to cook something for Baba's prasad as desired by him. But ?50 was too meagre an amount. What could I take back in such a small amount? So I searched through old wallets and opened up some untouched small savings of my house. After a lot of effort 1 managed to put together ?50 more. With a total of ?100,1 went to the market, shopped for the basic ingredients, came back home and cooked white grams (safed chana) for Baba's bhog with lots of love. Then with the ffhog Prasad in my hands, 1 went back to the Dwarkamai, where the old man was waiting for me. He was really happy with my hard work and sincerity The dish was first offered to Baba after the noon aarti and then distributed as prasad to the devotees. I felt so much at peace," she concluded.

The more I got to know Lalita, the more she amazed me. She had no money but had a heart so big that she even added her savings to the small amount given by the elderly man, in order to cook a substantial meal for Baba.

The elderly man smiled with affection, "You have made me very happy, my child. The dish you cooked was delicious. I want you to continue making delectable dishes tor offering at the Dwarkamai. From now on, prepare bhog worth ?200 every morning and ?20() every evening as offering for the next seven days, on my behalf. Use what you save to feed yourself and your family." Saying this he gave her the money to help her begin,

Lalita, who was very happy and excited at her new-found work, cooked new dishes at every meal... flattened rice (poiia), sweet rice (meethay chawal), salty rice (vegetable biryatti), sweets and desserts (haiwa') and so on. She would cook a large amount ofprasad and at the same time save some money for herself. Before she knew, her problems began disappearing; she now had enough to feed her family. But most important of all, she had got back her lost confidence and positive energy.

I am sure that in those four years of visiting Baba every morning with a delicious bhog, Lalita must have got Baba addicted to the divine taste of her hands! That is why He chose exactly the same profession for her. Lalita is supremely fortunate because for her... even literally... her work is worship.

The old man blessed her on the seventh day and was never seen again. Who was he? Where did he come from? And where did he go? No one knows anything. Words can't answer these questions but our hearts certainly can. Years have gone by ever since but he has never been seen again. The direction he gave to Lalita's life has led her out of her miseries. This blessing of the old man not only gave a new life to I.alita but also immensely benefitted devotees, who wished to abide by Baba's lesson of charity. All those keen on distributing food amongst the poor and needy or even amongst other devotees now only had to make a call to Lalita. She got quite a few orders on a daily basis and became a known name in Shirdi. People acknowledged her and respected her. The bhog cooked by her would he extraordinarily delicious. It fell as though she sprinkled her love and affection as condiments in the bttog, thereby adding a special, unknown flavour to it. She and her family now led a comfortable life. Her husband also assisted her in the noble work. All her children got admission in good schools and the entire family was blissfully happy by Baba's grace.
When 1 questioned her about the identity of the old man, she said to me with bright eyes, "He was my father, my Baba. 1 know that He was none other than my Sai. He came, showed me the path, blessed me and then went away." ☺

l,et me finally share how 1 met Ulita. 1 too wished to organize a bhandam (distribution of consecrated food) at Shirdi and a security officer introduced us. There was something very special about her. I think it was the blissful look on her face and the shimmer of Baba's love in her eyes. Clad in a brighi sari, smiling all the way, she first took me inside the Dwarkamai, where (he delicacies cooked by her were offered to Baba. Then she came back and mixed the consecrated *bhog* thus offered into the main dish. And finally, she helped me distribute the food to the huge gathering present outside the Dwarkamai, while her husband manned the crowd, keeping the large number of devotees in a queue to avoid any chaos and maintain decorum and harmony. I learnt the lesson of *Shraddha* and *Saburi* from her — of having faith and keeping it to the end, with unquestioned patience. She truly is Baba's daughter. So let us also keep our faith strong and our patience unswerving and always remember Baba's words of advice, **"These feet are old and holy. Whosoever takes refuge in them will be happy in this life and the next."**

My story was meant to end at that last line. But it is strange, actually a little eerie that Baba made me write down those last words, when 1 penned down this story in 2007: "Whosoever takes refuge in them [Baba's Holy Feet | will be happy in this life and the next." Little did 1 know that when I sat down to edit this beautiful miracle four years later, these words — which were somewhat prophetic — would have taken on a new meaning.

In 2011, when I visited Shirdi, as always I called Lalita to place my order. Her elder daughter received the call, "Yes, Didi (elder sister), please let me know what you want prepared and I'll meet you in the evening with the dish outside the Dwarkamai."

"That's very sweet, my dear. But I really wish to speak to your mother. It's been long and 1 have been missing her." 1 responded.

"Ohh!! *Didi,* you don't know??" she asked.

"Know what, my dear??" [asked, still wondering.

She paused, then continued, "Didi, Mama and Papa's scooter collided with a ti'jck, a few months back. They died on the spot."

My heart skipped a few beats. I didn't want to believe it. I just did not!! But, well, the truth was that I.alita had gone. She was barely in her early forties, may he younger. I have heard that God calls good people to Him very soon. And in Lalita's case, it wasn't just a beautiful human being but also a great cook. I won't be surprised if she cooks for her Father Sai, in heaven, where He had reserved a special place for her. As promised, Baba did accept her devotion and took her safely in His arms, over the seven seas.

I gathered my nerves after the phone call that day but I couldn't hold back my emotions that evening. Her daughter, a younger replica of her, waited for me with the dish of palm 1 had asked her to cook. While she and her younger sister helped me distribute the bhog, her brother took on their father's responsibility and manned the crowd.

My heart feels a deep prick even today when I write all this down. The children were carrying forth not only their parents' good work but also their name. Lalita has gone but her name is etched in our hearts forever, I pray that she is happy in her new world with her Baha Sai. Dressed in an elderly man's garb, Baba had not only given a direction to Lalita's life but also a livelihood to her kids because He knew that Lalita and her husband did not have many days. Such is our Baba, kind and foresighted. He plans for us far ahead of what we can ever imagine. Bless us, Baba, and keep us in Your Holy Feet forever. And we, in turn, promise to abide by the twin virtues of Faith and Patience. We promise to not lose hope, how much ever time it takes. **The door may take time to open... but the door surely will open.**

Prayer, devotion and complete faith in Baba's feet are the paramount virtues in a devotee but if these qualities are not accompanied by overflowing love, then these attributes are of no value. Pray to Him; give all your troubles to Him — but, at the same time, love Him. When we look at Baba's peerless form, His eyes overpower us with the profundity of love they behold. We must, in turn, reciprocate that love to Him... an endless flow of love from His eyes to ours and from ours to Him.

1 have heard people say, "Fear the Lord." (Bliagwan se daro, uske

keber se dam). But these words are totally baseless and false. How can we fear Him, who loves us the way no one does? Baba is Love Incarnate... He wards away all our troubles and works endlessly to remove every hurdle from our path, thereby making the journey of our life beautiful and blissful. Why should we fear Him? We should only love Him and trust Him. Prayer without love is like a diamond without lustre: it is both useless and worthless. Surrender to Baba reverentially. This is the easiest path to gain material and spiritual benefits while we are alive and attain salvation when we cast away our body. Love Him so much that you become one with Him and merge in Him forever.

Aum Sai Shri Sai faya Jaya Sai

"Rama (the God of the Hindus) and Rahim (the God of the Mohammedans) are one and the same; there is not the slightest difference between them; then why should their devotees quarrel among themselves"? Ton ignorant folks, join hands a-nd bring both the communities together, act sandy and thus you will gain your object of national unity. It is not good to dispute and argue. So don't argue, don't emulate others. Always consider your interest and welfare. The Lord will protect you. Yoga, sacrifice, penance, and knowledge are the means to attain God. If you do not succeed in this by any means, vain is your birth. If any one does any evil unto you, do not retaliate, if you can do anything, do some good unto others."

— SAI BABA OF SHIRDI

Baba's Priceless Lesson of Oneness

"You need not git far In seunh of Me. Barring your name and form, there exists In you, us well ax in ail beings, a sense of Being or Consciousness «/ Existence. That Is Myself. Knowing this, you see Me inside yourself, as well as In all beings, ff you practise this, you will realize my all-pervasiveness, and thus attain oneness with Me."

During Raha's Ilk', several discussions, controversies and debates came up, on whether Haba was a Hindu or a Muslim, He lived in a mosque, so He should In* Muslim; but lie called the mosque Dwarkamai, so He should be Hindu, His devotees celebrated the Muslim festival of Urus and took out the Sandal Procession but, on the very same day, the devotees also celebrated the Hindu festival of Ram Navami. He permitted Muslim devotees to say their narnaaz in His Dwarkamai and Hindu devotee's sari^ their aarti in Baba's masjid. On Baba's lips was "Allah Malik" (God is Supreme) but while repeating this, He would be busy in getting Hindu shrines repaired. He kept His Dhuni (sacred fire) ever burning like a devout Agnihotri (fire worshipper) Hindu and permitted all Hindu rituals and ceremonies in His Dwaikamai and yet respected every religion equally. But we foolish beings wanted to know Baba's religion, not realizing that He was far above these petty, meaningless discussions.

He who is God Incarnate... how can He be limited by a name, a form or a religion? He who lives within each of us as our Soul... how can He be a Hindu, a Muslim, a Sikh or a Christian? He whose single glance can alter the course of our destinies... how can He be given a restrictive label? He whose mere presence can destroy our sins accumulated over uncountable births... how can He be tied down by human confines of caste, colour or creed?

Our aim should be to attain the Divine Cosmic Oneness that Baba refers to. Our aim should be to merge in Him just as a drop blends into the ocean and loses itself in the vastness of that ocean. We must rise above these trivial and worthless arguments about Baba's background or religion. The heart only knows the language of love. It does not first enquire about religious bearing or cultura! demeanour. It only knows to love. Similarly, we must open our constricted mind to a wider world of love, light and spirituality, where God is formless, colourless, boundary-less and One.

Sagttn and Nirgun... Sakaar and Nirakaar... God with Form and God without Form... He does not lay guidelines on how to worship Him or in what form to worship Him. We decide, we choose and we carry out. The scriptures say that since we have a body and a form, we can begin with the worship of a God with l;orm *(Sagun).* It becomes easier to connect and identify when we attribute a body to the Lord God. And, once our devotion and the depth thereof grow apace, we can start worshipping His formless self *(Nirgan).* **He is the divinity within us, the goodness within us, the love within us. He is birth-less, death-less, time-less, space-less. He is the One Eternal Cosmic Soul... our Soul.**

And if we still have doubts in our mind, He has sent us an answer through His daughter Sophia. He has stepped into Sophia's world to show a path and give a direction to minds disillusioned by religious barriers.

I met Sophia when she came to my office looking for a job. There was something about her that held my gaze. She had one of the most charming faces I had ever come across. In addition, she had a serene disposition. One could almost see the glow of purity in her aura and all this at a time when she was going through the trauma of a divorce. The very first moment when I saw her is etched in my memory... a very young, attractive girl sitting on a couch, right at the comer of the reception area, accompanied by her fair, cute two-year-old son. I instantly bonded with her.

Sophia was born in a Christian family and grew up loving Jesus. She was a pious girl with boundless faith in Ghrist. Her childhood was spent visiting the church Sunday after Sunday and living the teachings of the priest. Then... after several years, both her life and her faith took a new turn. These were the days when she was studying at a college in Delhi. As luck would have it — or perhaps destiny — she happened to accompany a college friend to a temple on Lodhi Road in Delhi.

She had no idea what or where she was headed to. "My friend wanted to visit a temple, so I tagged along," she smiled, as she took me back, down memory lane. "Chatting busily, we walked up the stairs of the temple and then as I looked right in front, I froze. Glued to the eyes that looked at me from a beautiful idol, I stood still... and my world stood still." Saying this, she paused for a few moments. I could clearly see her submerged in a sea of emotions, finding it hard to speak. "1 could not take my eyes off Him. 1 felt a surge of energy inside me, which soon melted into tears. 1 found myself frantically thinking, 'Who is He?? Why am I crying??'" Her eyes lit up, "It was strange that even before I could know His name, I was in love with Him. I turned towards my friend and asked, 'Who is He?' She smiled back, 'He is Sai Baba of Shirdi.'"☺

And that marked the beginning of a fresh chapter in Sophia's life. Baba came to her at a time when she needed Him the most. Unfortunately, life for her had always been a struggle. She had lost her parents at a very early age and then lived through the emotional ordeal of a broken marriage. She had no family to support her through the hell that she was going through. Times were tough but Baba became her strength and her little son Jehaan became her reason to survive. Baba's timely entry into her world gave life a new meaning and gave her new reasons to smile despite the thorns in her path.

Sophia loved Baba but then slie loved Christ too. She had grown up holding Christ's hand but today she was holding on to Baba's hand as well.

As Sophia said, "At times I felt guilty of not being fair to either. 1 questioned my own faith. When I spent hours meditating on Baba and dwelling on His love, 1 opened my eyes to Christ and then felt very unsure if I was on the right path."

Life went on with Sophia always trying to maintain a balance between her devotion to her childhood friend Christ and her new-found love Sai,

1 am sure Baba must have been smiling at His child's plight and that of many others like Sophia. We all know that God is One. We all know that by whatever name we may call Him or in whatever form we may worship Him, our prayers reach just one Absolute Power... a Power that has no form, no name... a Power that is Pure Light and Divinity. But our religious conditioning is such that despite knowing reality, we still develop doubts, apprehensions and, at times, even guilt. So also was the case with Sophia. Her state might have been hidden from the world but it was certainly not hidden from her Baba.

One night as Sophia slept, she had a dream. There were two groups of people at a small distance from each other. She could heat both the groups chanting slogans, loud and clear. One group was shouting out in unison, "Praise be to Jesus." And the other group was incessantly chanting, "Jai Sai Ram." Sophia stood at the centre, totally lost and unsure, as to which way to go. She took one step towards the group that was repeating the name of Christ. Then halted and turned towards the group of people intoning Baba's name. "Which way should 1 go?" she screamed in anguish. Then as she stood deeply distraught and troubled, she felt a movement in the crowd that was repeating Baba's name.

And behold! To her surprise and joy, she saw dear Baba walking out towards her from the centre of the group. As she stood in awe, mesmerized by the halo around Him, He smiled at her tenderly and spoke, "Why do you trouble yourself unnecessarily by thinking so much? Do not worry and stay peaceful at heart. **Realize the fact that Jesus and I are One. There is no difference between us. Take**

any one name and it is equivalent to worshipping the other. I AM YOUR JESUS FROM SHIRDI." Saying this, He placed His boon bestowing hand on Sophia's head and took her along with Him, hack to the devotees, who had now merged together into one, single group. ☺

Baba reaffirmed once again that He dwells in every fragment of the Universe. He is the One God Almighty. We know Him by different names, worship Him in different forms but He is the One Supreme Absolute. **All He wants from His devotees is to take His name with love and pure-hearted devotion. And He runs out to His children, irrespective of which name was called out. An honest prayer could be made to Sai or Nanak, Ram or Kahim, Jesus or Krishna; but the answer will come from the same One Power, One Soul, One Pammatma, One God....**

Hundreds of rivers flow into the ocean and lose their names and forms. So also, a man of wisdom and intellect gets rid of his identification to his name and his form and becomes one with the Supreme Reality.

The Upanishads explain this beautiful existence of the Supreme Absolute with the example of the electric current. The human eye cannot see the electric current or the electricity that flows through the wires. It only becomes visible to us when it assumes a body, a conductor or a contour. It takes the farm of a fan when in movement and it manifests as light when in a bulb; it emits sound and light as a microwave when it heats and it assumes the name of 'A refrigerator when it cools. But in the midst of all these different shapes, sizes, names and forms, the current remains unchanged. Seeing the light in the bulb ot the movement of the fan does not imply that we can see the electric current. We cannot even make out the presence or the absence of this current by looting at s naked wire or cable... till it sparks or till the time we turn on the switch, which controls its flow to the fan 01 the bulb.

Similarly, the Life Centre or the Awareness in us is formless in nature and cannot be seen by our eye. But once the switch of inner wisdom and knowledge is turned on, we become aware of its Divine Existence within us. The outer envelopment of matter is subject to birth and death but the Supreme was never horn and it can never die. This auspicious, non-dual, self-luminous Absolute is our dear Baba... our Sai.

Aum Sai Shri Jaya Jaya Sai

"Though I am a Fakir, have no house or wife, and though, leaving fill care, 1 stay at one place, the inevitable Maya teases Me often. Though I forgot Myself but she cannot forget Me. She always envelops Me. This Maya (illusive power) of the Lord (Shri Hari) teases even God Brahma and others, then what to speak of a poor Fakir, like Me? Those who take refuge in the Lord will be freed from her clutches with His grace."

— SAI BABA OF SHIRDI

The Final Journey - To Baba, With Baba

"He, who remembers Me in his last moments, conies verily to Me, and he that meditates otherwise, at that time, goes to what he looks for."

Lord Shri Krishna has said in the iihugwad (Ufa that saints are no different from Him. They are His living, breathing form. The aura, the energy and the presence of saints is so pious, so powerful that even the most sacred rivers like the Ganga, Yamuna and Saraswati, which cleanse the sins of millions of people every day, look forward to be consecrated by their holy feet. These rivers are vertly goddesses and a dip in their waters has the potency to rid us of our sins accumulated over several lifetimes. Yet, they await the touch of the saint's feet because such gratifying presence in turn purifies and empowers their holy waters. If saints are so adulated, in what words do I describe the all-powerful, enigmatic presence of dear Baba, who was not a mere saint but God Incarnate?

Baba's life was like a waterfall that rejuvenated and refreshed the surroundings, gave life to many plants and trees, quenched the thirst of millions and finally disseminated into several rivers that carried forward this life-giving task slarted by Baba. And every **life He touched was illumined; every person He met was purified; every disease He glanced at was cured; every dying person who took refuge at His feet got salvation. Such is the grandeur of dear Baba's presence.** He not only benefitted His devotees in life but made sure that their final moments were momentous and their final path laden with blessings.

Scriptures stand witness to the truth that whatever are the last thoughts of a man on his deathbed, he is born to the same in his next life. There's a very interesting story of a rich merchant that I once heard.

This merchant is taking his last few breaths and is about to die, when he screams aloud, "Where is my eldest son?"

"To your right, Father," responds the son.

"And what about my youngest one?"

"I am to your left, Father."

"Oh, I am dying, where is my third and most beloved son?"

"Father, dear Father, I am at your feet," says his third boy.

At this, the father roars in anguish, "You idiots! All three of you are here. Then who is taking care of the business at my shop?" Saying these last words, he dies. And guess what, he takes his next birth very soon — as a dog outside his own shop (the merchant's shop). ©

Baba. who was an embodiment of the Vedas, knew this truth very well. So He always told His devotees to keep taking God's name all the time. His advice was that if you habitually chant the name of the Lord, then at the final moments of your life, the remembrance of God will come to you naturally and without much effort. Then our mind will not go to bodily attachments but will merge in the Lord. Several saints, sages, holy men and even animals breathed their last at Baba's feet. What could be better than leaving this world at the feet of your Guru, your God, Sai Baba? This ensured an illumined path for their soul and secured them salvation.

The kind Baba, who could see the past, present and future of His children, knew beforehand if their death was approaching. When living in Shirdi, Baba advised many such devotees to read the seriptures day and night, and to meditate on God, without giving them I IIP slightest Indication that their end was near. Little did these people know Ki.it our kind Baba was clearing their road to the next world. In liirl, when the time had come for Baba Himself to leave this world, He asked a devotee named Mr Vaze to read the Holy Scriptures in His presence. Mr Vaze read them before Baba for about 15 days, after which Baba passed away. Baba, who was God Himself, did not need such a reading or salvation. But to leave a positive message for His devotees, He laid an example with His own life. Such was our soft-hearted, compassionate Baba. And it did not stop at that. He continues coming into the lives of His children, even today, at the right time, and makes sure that they are not alone or lonely in their last moments. Sometimes, He draws them out from the jaws of death and at other times, accompanies them to their final destination. What I am about to share with you is very close to my heart. It took my breath away when it occurred years ago and the very thought of it makes my heart beat out of rhythm even today,

A wonderful human being, an extremely warm and affectionate person and an ardent devotee of Sai Baba... this is a brief description of my dear friend Deepak Sharma. I first met him on an official visit. I had my business at that time and Deepak was working as the HR Manager with one of my client organizations. Initially It was a purely professional relationship but soon we hit it off really well together and became acquainted at a more personal level. Deepak was a very humhle, down-to-earth, soft-hearted young man from Jammu. He was so simple, so unpretentious that I almost felt he was a misfit in a metro like Delhi. Another very strong reason that enhanced our bonding was the presence of dear Baba in our lives. We used to spend most of our lime together talking about Baba and His *leelas.*

At this time, Deepak was going through some financial problems. He had started a part-time business which failed miserably and so now he tiail to pay back debts amounting to huge sums of money. He had no resources other than his salary and that was just not enough. But he had tremendous faith in Baba's feet and this faith gave him the courage to move on in life and bravely withstand all problems and adversities.

Time flew... Deepak got married to a pretty girl from the hills and was soon blessed with a beautiful baby daughter. He also got promotions due to his hard work and good nature and joined a new organization at a senior managerial position. Slowly but steadily, he continued to pay back his debts and finally managed to pay them off completely. So life could not have been better. No tensions, no debts, a caring wife and a delightful little daughter; be could not have asked for more. Dccpak's faith in Baba grew stronger and deeper.

Deepak wanted to formally introduce me to his boss in the new organization so that I could start a business association with him here as well. I still remember very clearly, it was October, 2004. He asked me to come over to his office for a meeting on 18th October. 1, very smartly and tactfully, requested him to postpone it to 19th October on the pretext of some other important appointment. Actually, it was Deepak's birthday on 19th October and he was under the impression that I had forgotten the occasion. So I wanted to surprise him with flowers and wishes, and I thought I could do so when I reached his office for the meeting. Accordingly, Deepak, in all his innocence, postponed my meeting with his boss and I was really excited and eager to give him a surprise on his birthday.

I first decided to take flowers for him but then 1 thought that it may not be appropriate as I was visiting him during office hours. Then I recalled (by Baba's grace, I guess) a recent conversation with Deepak in which he had told me that he had no idea as to what was the *Shri Sai Satcharita.* 1 was quite surprised that in so many years of knowing Baba, he had never come across this holy book which is equivalent to the Bhagwad Cita for Baba's devotees. The *Shri Sai Satcharita* is not a book. It is verily Baba Himself... imparting knowledge and instructions, showing the path to a righteous life and fulfilling the needs and wishes of His devotees. All this and much more is possible through the *Shri Sai Satcharita.* So 1 decided that there could be no better gift for Deepak on his birthday as I knew that he was eager to the extent of desperation to Ht'l hi ild of n copy. 1 always keep a large stock of Baba's pictures, idols and copies of the *Shri Sai Satcharita* at home, to gift to my friends. So on iln- morning of the 19th, I took along with me a beautiful idol of Baba and the *Shri Sai Satcharita* and reached Decpak's office for the meeting.

We were sitting in the conference room when I handed over the auspicious gifts to him and wished him a happy birthday. He was delighted as he had presumed that I had forgotten his special day. And when he saw the gifts, he just could not stop smiling. In fact, he looked like an excited kid who had got a box of chocolates that he had wanted desperately! Deepak then and there started reading the *Shri Sai Satcharita.* I sat in silence, smiling at his child-like exuberance, while I waited for his hoss to arrive. Deepak appeared to have forgotten that I was sitting next to him and just kept turning the pages randomly and reading the book. After quite some time, he went out with Baba's idol and the *Shri Sai Satcharita* and placed them on the desk in his cubicle, fl could see the desk from the glass door of the conference room.) I remember looking at Baba sitting there on the table top, as I smiled to myself and wondered, "Baba, You have come to Deepak on a very special day. So what are You planning? I'm sure You have some very special reason for coming to him today." Baba did answer my question very soon. You will realize what I mean as you read on.

Anyway, I had a very good meeting and when I was bidding goodbye to Dipak, he informed me that he would be leaving early next morning with his wife and daughter to attend a wedding in another city. He told me that I could start my new project with his organization after a week when he came back. I wished him good iuck and a safe journey and drove off.

Late that night he called me up in an excited voice, "Guess what! I've spent the entire day reading Baba's *Satcharita* and I'm going to read more through the night. I just love it and can't take my eyes off it. Thanks a lot for the gift. I'll treasure it till my last breath." I smiled happily.

It was 21st October. My family and 1 were very busy as it was Durga *Axhtami,* a very auspicious day for Hindus. Prasad was being prepared for the Kanjak Puja (prayer) that is carried out on Ashtami (little girls are worshipped on this day and offered food and gifts). It also happened to be a Thursday, which is considered Baba's day. So, like every other Thursday, Baba's beautiful marble idol in our house was lielng bathed with milk, honey, curd, sugar and rose water. Our house k'lt and smelt like a Holy Shrine.

Everything was going on well by Baba's grace and just as the puja was coming to an end, my phone rang. It was a call from Deepak's office. One of his colleagues whom 1 had met on the day of our meeting, was on the line.

"Ma'am, would you have any other contact number of Deepak other than his cell phone?"

"I am afraid, I don't," I responded. "But why do you need it? What happened? Is everything all right?"

"Ma'am, we tried calling Deepak for some work-related issue but his phone is being received by some strange person. He says that the phone is with the police as Deepak's car has met with an accident."

I was shocked, speechless; and when I finally spoke, there were endless ijiit'stions, "What?? Accident?? Oh my God!! How is Deepak? Is he okiiy? Who all were in the car?"

"We have no idea, Ma'am, and that is why we called you hoping that you'll have some other contact number as you've known him for years," he replied.

At lilts, I told him that I had no other contact number but I would try and call some other friends who may have it and get back to him as soon as I could. My head was spinning; I was absolutely blank. But I gathered my nerves and started calling al! common friends to look for Deepak's number. One friend assured me that he would get back with the number soon. I was anxious and worried. I closed my eyes and started praying to Baba.

I was praying intently, eyes closed, deep in meditation when someone shook me up. I jumped up and looked around. But to my surprise, my room was empty. There was no one next to me. Then who shook me? As I sat back bewildered, 1 felt as if someone was there near mt, looking at me. But then it was only a feeling, a very strange feeling that I had never felt before in my life. I don't know why, but I suddenly felt as if it was Deepak. God!! 1 can probably never put in words what I felt at that moment. I still shiver at the powerful yet painful memory as I write this. I clearly recall that despairing moment... 1 remember feeling not just perturbed but sick with an unknown fear. I sunk deeper into my chair and looked at Baba's huge picture next to me, not knowing what to do. Where was Deepak? Why was 1 getting this uneasy feeling? Was it merely my fear? Why was my fear 'feeling' so real? I hoped that Deepak and his family were safe. I prayed to Baba that even if they had met with an accident, there should only be minor injuries and nothing worse. But what had shocked the life out of me was that strange feeling. I was meditating on Baba and someone disrupted the meditation. Why did I still feel as if someone was trying to convey something to me?

I was still looking at Baba's picture and in complete panic, my hands trembling, I picked up Baba's Satcltarita and prayed, "Baba, I am randomly going to open any page of the Satcharita. Please give me a hint or message about Deepak and his family's well-being."

1 did this often. Actually, 1 still continue this practice. Whenever in doubt, I pray to Baba and open the Shri Sai Satcharita and it is amazing that 1 always get an answer to my query in direct or indirect words. So, even on that day 1 did the same. I closed my eyes, prayed and opened the Sai Satcharita. The first words I read were, Tatyasaheb Noolkar gave up his ghost in Shirdi.' Gave up his ghost??

That means he passed away in Shirdi!! ("fttyasaheb was an ardent devotee of Baba who loved Baba dearly and finally breathed his last at His Holy Feet). I could feel tears pricking in my eyes. My vision was blurred. What was Baba trying to tell me? This could not be true. Was he using Tatyasaheb's name in place of Deepak's name? Deepak could not have left us and gone forever. Why did Baba take out this page and this page only? Why??

I prayed aloud, "Baba, please explain clearly, please, Baba," and then I read further, 'As Tatyasaheb's end was approaching, sacred literature was read out to him.' Sacred literature!! Oh God! Is that why Baba made me take the *Sai Satcharita* to Deepak? Was Baba preparing him for his final journey? My mind was in a state that I can't possibly put into words. But then I knew by now that something was seriously wrong because Baba's *Satcharita* would never lie.

My phone rang. True to Baba's word, the news that I hated to accept had finally come. Deepak had left us forever. His car had a head-long collision with a train. He was alone in the car at that time. He had gone to never come back again. So Deepak was now a part of our memories, only memories. And because of our bonding through Baba, he had halted on his way to Baba's abode in heaven and shaken me up in my meditation to tell me that he was going. 1 had 'felt' him. It was and still remains my life's most inexplicable moment... I had sensed at that wry moment... that Deepak was around. When souls are bonded by divinity... we have such soulful experiences. He must have wanted to siiy goodbye, the final goodbye. He must have wanted to say, "Aum Sai Ham. I am going forever."

I learnt my lessons that day. I learnt about the depth of Sai's love. This traumatic experience taught me that if we love Baba with a pure heart, III1 not only looks after us in life but also ensures salvation for us in (It'iilh. He knew that Deepak was nearing his end and so He made sure Unit the last days of his life were spent in reading sacred literature; His vrry own Sai Satcharita, which according to accepted beliefs ensures salvation after death. He reached Deepak in the nick of time and accompanied him in his final journey. Such is our Baba, kind and softhearted. He is with us always — everywhere — in life and even after life. He opens the doors of heaven for those children who love Him and trust Him.

Whenever in pain or anxiety, hold the Satcharita close to your heart and you will experience peace and bliss. Interminable, infallible and unquestionable is the power of the Sat Satcharita. One who reads it daily, little by tittle, will get alt that he desires or prays for. The Sai Satcharita is Baba's most beautiful gift to His children. It is like a magic wand. Ask, read, pray and all your wishes shall be fulfilled. You will get bliss in life and salvation in death. Deepak went away hut taught us the depth with which we should trust our God. He taught us the meaning of pure love for OUT Gum. **For anyone who loves His Lord God with purity, selflessness and innocence is never forsaken, never left alone... not in life, not in death.** My prayers for you, my dear friend Deepak.,.. You have gone away forever but left behind a great lesson of true faith and devotion. May you shine in the sky as an angel star... till eternity.

Aum Sai Shri Sai faya Jaya Sai

"If I take one rupee as Dakshina from anybody I have to return it tenfold to him. J never take anything gratis. I never ask any one indiscriminately. I only ask and take from him whom the Fakir (My Guru) points out. If anyone is indebted formerly to the Fakir, money is received from him. The donor gives, i.e., sows his seeds, only to reap a rich harvest in future. Wealth should, be the means to work out Dharma. If it is used for personal enjoyment, it is wasted. Unless you have given it before, you do not get it now. So the best way to receive is to give. The giving of Dakshina *advances* Vairagya *[non-attachment] and thereby* Bhakti *and* Cyan. *Give one and receive tenfold."*

— SAI BABA OF SHIRD!

The Miraculous Power of Charity

Charity given In a holy place and to a holy personage conduces to the donor's welfare. What is more holy than Shirdi and its Presiding Deity, Sai Baba?

Charity was very close to Baba's heart. All His life, all He possessed was given away in charity to His devotees. Thousands of rupees were given to Baba over His lifetime as dakshina but Baba in turn gave away every penny to His devotees. When Baba passed away, it is said that despite having received a huge amount of money as dakshina, only a meagre amount — ?16 —was found in His possession. Such was Baba's love for charity. And this charity was not through money alone as He also encouraged the giving away of food as the best form of charity. So wonderful was Baba's love that when He decided to distribute food, He cooked with His own loving hands and fed all His devotees to their heart's content. Right from buying the ingredients, to grinding, pounding, chopping and cooking, He did it all Himself. Then, the food cooked by Baba was consecrated by making an offering to God and finally served to His children. Knowing Baba's love for charity, we, as His children must walk the same path and do the same service.

Baba not only emphasized the importance of charity in human life but also gave valid, justifiable reasons as to why charity must be practised. He said that charily always provides for the donor's welfare. Like the crown has a pinnacle that adds to its glory, so also charity is at the pinnacle of all virtues. The highest form of charity as preached by Baba is unnadaan, ic, the giving of food. **He taught in His special way that one must first offer food to the Lord before partaking of it. And it would be even more gratifying and conducive to the**

individual if, after making an offering to God, the poor, the needy and the disabled are offered a meal.

From the well-known adage 'As you sow, so shall you reap', it can be interpreted that we must perform good actions in our live? if we want good results in return. But this is a very superficial interpretation of an extremely profound thought. If we delve deeper and bring out the philosophical significance underlying this saying, it would entail that our present and future are nothing but an outcome or end result of our past. The word 'past', in Vedic terms, would refer to innumerable, uncountable past births that each soul has experienced. These experiences are created due to our big and small karmas. Each karma either adds to the positive or the negative balance that we hold, in God's bank. Each good act brings forth joy, health, success and bliss whereas each wrongdoing results in sorrow, disease, failure and suffering.

A question may be asked here that if our today and tomorrow are dependent 011 infinite actions of our uncountable births, then are we not slaves bound by the limitations of our own past karmas? And if we are bound, then how can we transform our future for the better? If we are predestined to suffer due to past karmas, then what can we, meek human beings, do to bring about a change, in the future course of our lives?

"Stop worrying," says Baba. "When I am here to guide you, why do you fear? I will wipe away the negative impact of all your past life karmas. You are my children and will 1 ever let your future be drowned in sorrow? No, I will not. So, 1 promise to amend your present and future but I can't do it without your help. All you have to do is think good thoughts, do good actions, feed the hungry and clad the naked. And 1 promise to take care of the rest. If you have wealth, feed as many as possible with as much as you can. But if you don't have enough or are living in scarcity, even then don't worry... share your little meal with the needy, just share or give away a few morsels of love, because little thoughtful acts have the power to eradicate

uncountable negatives of past Karmas and replenish your dishes with abundance and your house with joy. So give, share and care and you will see happy miracles in your life each moment, each day."

Baba continues with a smile, "Wealth should be the means to work out Dharnia. If you have given it before you get it now. And give it now, if you want to receive it in your future. Give with love, with empathy, with joy. If the thought that accompanies an act of giving is positive, joyful and selfless, then the impact of such an act in the individual's life assumes unparalleled magnitude. The outcome becomes life-transforming. So give with love, with joy and with magnanimity. Give because you derive happiness from giving and not because you want to receive. You will receive in both cases, but when you give without being bound by the result or fruit of your actions, then the positive impact on your life is manifold, of what it would have been, had you given only to receive returns of such meaningful acts. The meaning is lost from the meaningful acts if demeaning limitations are attached to them. So, give. Charity in any form conduces to the donor's welfare. But the highest form of charity is the giving away of food. Feed the starving and I shall feed you for all your future births to come."

Baha's words touch my soul. They arc so powerful, so captivating. They remind me of Sudama's story. SuiJama once lied to Lord Krishna when they were living together in their Guru Sandipani's ashram. Sudama ate the grams given by their Guru's wife all alone without sharing them with Krishna and told Him that the Mother had not given any grams to him at all. As a result of this act of eating alone, he lived in acute poverty for years to come. But when his wife cooked parched rice with lots of love for Lord Shri Hari and offered it to Him, He blessed them with a golden city in return. So making an offering of food is the highest form of charity. But just giving in the human form is not enough. First make an offering unto His divine feet, then serve others and finally serve yourself with it. fs He not with us at every moment, day or night? Then why starve Him? So first offer food to llaba, feed Him with love and then serve His children with it. Such food becomes nectar and contributes to the health and happiness of all those who partake of it. So let us make a promise, never to eat alone... to share with Baba and also with His children.

My life has been connected to the virtue of charity in a very divine, special way. 'I am' because of 'charity'. As strange as it may sound, I owe my very existence to this life-giving virtue. I can't help but become emotional even before 1 begin to narrate this story of my life. It is the story of why I am in this world today, despite the declaration by doctors and science that I would not be born at all... that my mother should not even attempt to conceive me... that even if she did conceive and if I were to be born, I would not survive. But I am very much here, alive and breathing, because dear God had different plans. ☺

1 am not writing this little miracle to narrate to you how and why I was born. 1 am writing this to share a great lesson with you, which, by far, is the greatest lesson I have personally learnt in life and about life. 1 promise you that reading this story could be life-transforming for you. If what you learn is followed with a pure heart, no goal shall remain unachievable, no dream unattainable... and the little mantra that I share with you is the easiest to practise as well, baba's lesson of charity reflects my entire life, like a mirror. I see the power in this virtue, the power to recreate, rewrite destinies.

My parents had been married for more than seven years when I was born. It wasn't as though 1 was born late; rather, it happened because my Maa gave birth to three lovely, handsome boys — Komi, Sachit and Kajit — before I was born. I am told by one and all that they were among the cutest, healthiest and happiest babies one could have ever come across. They lit up my Maa and I'apa's life with their laughter, only to leave a dead silence behind. My parents lost them to the cruel hands of destiny, one after the other. If writing this after almost forty years of their having gone makes my heart shiver, I am left to wonder what my Maa and Papa must have gone through.

All three babies were absolutely well, with no health conditions or complaints whatsoever. Doctors had no clue why they suddenly collapsed In Maa's arms. The youngest. Rajit, was only seven days old when he succumbed to fate. He was happily playing with Maa, who was still recouping in hospital after his binh. After some time, he fell silent and she thought he was asleep. When she touched him affectionately, he was ice-cold. Before she knew it, he had gone. My Papa was then fighting the 1971-war against Pakistan, since he was an officer in the Indian Armed Forces. He could not even be informed at the borders as telecommunication was not so advanced back then. So, when he came back with toys and gifts {as he knew my Maa was due any time), all he got was a grieving, shattered wife, who had just lost her third son. Papa didn't even see him. He had gone before Papa could have held his little tiny son in his arms. I can't hold back my tears or stop my hands from trembling when I write this even after so many years and that too when I have never seen or met all these older brothers and was not a Jiving part of this bitter, painful experience. I am compelled to think again and again, what must have been the plight of my parents who had lost three sans in the first five years of their marriage, aged 2lfi, 1V4 and one week. They had lost the first two before having the third one... but he too didn't stay.

Papa is a wonderful man. He did all he could to keep Maa busy, post this traumatic episode. He enrolled her into various hobby courses to keep her mind occupied. Me took her on holidays and vacations despite his own sorrowful state and Maa also .started staying happy for Papa's happiness. They knew that, after all, they were the 'only' source of happiness in each other's lives and this was to be true for the rest of their lives too... as doctors had added to their trauma of losing three sons by declaring that they should not take the risk of planning a baby ever again. Medical science had not progressed so much hack then. But to put in simple words, what the doctors said was that if Maa and Papa by luck had a son again, chances of his survival would be very bleak. In case they had a daughter she just may survive, though they could give no assurance for that either. To avoid another tragic episode — since choosing a boy or a girl was beyond their control — they decided to never plan a baby and may be, at a later stage, adopt a child.

Around a year and a half went by. Maa and Papa were slowly getting better, though not any happier, when a stranger visited their house. He had been referred by Papa's colleague for some work.

After finishing his work, he spoke to Papa, "Sir, i have heard about your tragedy. 1 want to request you to come with me to a very saintly soul called Kambli Vaale Babaji. I am sure He will bless you with a baby. Please, sir, do come along with Ma'am."

My parents were the last people to resort to any such method as they had very strong faith in God but not in astrologers, pandits or any human descendants of God. They thanked the gentleman and politely refused to go with him. But what is fated must happen, I guess, and so this man didn't give up. He kept visiting my parents off and on, and kept urging them to come with him just once. He was so persistent — and since he had nothing to gain personally in the entire situation — Maa and Papa finally conceded before his goodness. And so they went to meet Kambli Vaale Babaji.

Though 1 talk about Kambli Vaale Babaji in this story, to me he is no different from my dearest Sai Babaji. I know for sure that all holy souls that have stepped into this world and taken different human forms may look and appear to be different but they are all One Divine Light. They have all taken birth — in human form — for us... to take us on the righteous path, to guide us when we falter and to give us strength when we waiver. I must be so fortunate to have always had aged, holy hands of blessing on my head and that too of lovely, sweetheart Babaj),1;, one after the other. It was, as though, they had pre-decided to keep coming into my life and taking care of me, especially when ! needed them the most. Their names and forms don't matter, for their soul is the Cosmic Soul, God's soul. So, this story of my life is not a digression from Sai Babaji, but is only an add-on to His marvellous leelas.

Kambli means blanket and this Babaji wrapped only a blanket around himself, be it heat or cold and hence the name Kambli Vaale Babaji. He was around 90 years of age, had almost no vision, could only walk with help hut I am told he had the glow of youth on his face and plumpy reel ness In his cheeks. Those days, he lived in an old bungalow, which belonged to some devotee as he had no permanent place of stay. When my parents reached the bungalow, they were surprised to see very renowned personalities sitting among the devotees. The then Prime Minister of India, very senior officials, chiefs of the Armed Forces, etc, used to come regularly to seek Babaji's blessings. And many famous personalities of the Mumbai (then Bombay) film fraternity were also regulars at Babaji's place,

Maa and Papa sat down at the back of the room. They did not approach Babaji. A few hours went by and Maa started getting very anxious. As she was beckoning Papa to leave, she heard Babaji call out to someone, "Puttar, mere kol act." (Child, come to me.)

Maa looked up, wondering who he was calling out to and was taken by surprise to see everyone turning back to look at her. Devotees signalled to her, "Babaji is calling you. Please move up closer." (Don't forget what I mentioned before... Babaji couldn't see... and Maa was anyway too far for his diminishing vision.)

Maa and Papa moved up. No one had yet introduced them to Babaji. As they sat down at his feet, he spoke to Maa, "You have lost all you had before coming here, my child. You have lost all three."

At this, Maa, obviously taken aback by shock at how he knew everything and also overcome by emotion and painful memories, broke down before him.

Babaji continued, "What do the doctors say? They say you will never have a baby? You surely will, my child. Some people get happiness early in life and some late. There is a lot of happiness in store for you, a little lale though. But it is there. So stop crying. God will do good."

Then he smiled at Papa and looked back at Maa, "My Fauji Puttar (Soldier Son) is a wonderful man. He will look after you well. So smile now."

Maa and Papa tell me even today how calming and soothing were his words. They didn't want to be there just a few moments ago and now they didn't feel like leaving. But he blessed them and asked them to come another day.

My sweethearts, Maa and Papa, were looking forward to seeing Babaji again. On arriving at Babaji's abode on the next visit, they observed his kindness and love. Devotees were being served endless rounds of tea and snacks. There were arrangements for food to be served to one and all, too. And Babaji wanted nothing from his children but joyful smiles on their faces. Decisions of national importance were taken by many people holding powerful positions but only in consultation with Babaji. The who's who of the world were at Babaji's feet but for him all weie the same. He saw no difference between a king and a pauper and loved everyone equally. This quality was innate to Sai Babaji as well. The richest and the poorest were treated as equals in Baba's court.

That day, Babaji took Maa and Papa aside and sat down with them in solitude. He then repeated to them words that Sai Baba too has repeated incessantly to all those who have sought His blessings. "My children, do all the good you can, in all the ways you can, to all the people you can and even to as many animals as you can." As Maa and Papa looked on, he continued, "Feed the poor, clad the naked, give water to the thirsty. Do as much charity as you can. Do as much good to this world as you can. My blessings are with you." Maa and Papa asked no questions, smiled at him in gratitude, took Babaji's blessings and left.

For the next few months, they just did what Babaji had advised them to do. They went regularly to orphanages and homes for children and fed them to their heart's content. They visited homes for widows (I didn't even know that back in those years even such places existed) and took clothes and food foi the women. Maa and Papa planted several hundreds of fruit trees and prayed that years later when these trees bore fruit, they would satiate the hunger of several starving souls. They got drinking water taps and water tanks fixed at various places on the streets to quench the thirst of people who moved in the scorching sun. They went to places where cows are fed and bred to provide milk. They carried with them cow-food and fed several cows so that they would give healthy, pure milk. The list is endless: I can go on and on. But I leave it to the readers to figure out other ways of charity and kindness. Maa and Papa also visited a few shrines and holy places and sought blessings as guided by Babaji. And I must mention here that these holy places were of no single religion. They went to temples, gurmiwaras, dargahs, churches and so on. And as they tell me, they had no clue why Babaji had asked them to do so — but they asked no questions. Whatever they did, gave them immense joy and a calmness within. As Papa says, "We did all that we did because we loved every bit of it. There can be no greater joy than that of bringing a smile on sad lips."

During this period, they visited Bahaji as well and took an active part in cooking for and feeding his devotees. Maa tells me several interesting events witnessed by Dad and her. One day, cooking and feeding was going on at a large scale when devotees realized that there were no hags of flour left in the bungalow. They softly whispered this into Babaji's ears and he insisted that they had not checked properly. So the devotees went back and checked again and again but the store was absolutely empty. At this Bahaji insisted they take him inside. And when they helped Babaji into the store, they were aghast to see Babaji smiling and pointing at several bags of flour lying in there! No one knows till date where the bags came from. © On another day, a very small quantity of cooked lentils was left and loo many guests were still left to he served. There was no time to cook again as people had already started eating. When Bahaji came to know of this, he asked to be taken into the kitchen. Once there, he dipped his bare arm into the boiling cauldron and started stirring it with his hand. And soon the cauldron was full, up to the brim, Maa and Papa are witness to this and several other amazing incidents. And the world is witness to similar stories of our dear Sai Baha as well. ©

Maa and Papa continued doing the good work they were advised to do, as and when they got time. (They tell me they made it a point to do so at least twice every week). At the same time, they visited Babaji regularly and in Papa's words, "We gained so much just by being close to him. His aura was so powerful. Merely being in his presence gave us peace in our hearts and the strength to move on. He never asked us for anything. All he wanted from us was that we should keep doing lots of kind acts of charity and have firm faith that all will be well."

Almost a year went by. There were occasions when Maa-1'apa observed Bahaji conveying to them in a subtle, discreet manner, "All will be well. Now there is nothing to worry. Lots of happiness lies ahead. Have faith." And then one day, over a conversation, they felt that Bahaji was giving them a signal that they could now plan a baby without any concern or anxiety. So, with complete faith on Babaji and a vibrant feeling of joy and fulfilment due to the many acts of kindness and charity they had carried out, they went ahead with a million prayers and a baby was conceived. ☺

When Babaji heard the good news, he was obviously very happy. At the same time, he asked Mum and Dad to continue the charities and in Maa's fifth month of pregnancy, he asked them to visit a very famous shrine and plant five fruit trees in its garden, which they did. Maa read a lot of scriptures and spiritual books during this period and both of them prayed that their baby should be a girl child. They desperately wanted a daughter.

Maa's eighth month of pregnancy was drawing to an end when she had a dream. She saw herself flying in the air, drifting from temple to temple, shrine to shrine. There were incense sticks all around and her dream almost smelt of them. And then behold!! She saw Babaji there. He stretched out his arm and gave her the prasacl of fruit and smilingly asked her to consume all of it herself and not share it with anyone. And Maa says that she woke up the next morning and told Dad, "it's going to be a girl." The experience of Maa's dream was so real and powerful that it left hei brimming with positivity and a feeling that it would be a girl.

And a girl it was!! ☺

Thanks to Babaji's blessings and my most wonderful Maa and Papa's unceasing prayers and goodness, I was born. ! am told that on top of my birth papers at the hospital were written the two words 'Precious Child.' And trust me, only my heart knows how precious I feel. Words fail me, each time I wish to thank my angel parents. Their countless good deeds before my birth and their love that taught me righteous living, imbibed in me morality and embedded in me deep within the virtues of goodness, truthfulness, discipline and charity, making me what I am today. I am what I am only because of them. And yes, the blessings didn't stop at me. God blessed them with another precious angel after another nine years... my younger sister, my baby Neha.

I have poured my heart out on paper... not because I wanted to share the story of my coming into this world with you. No!! Not at all!! That isn't the reason at all. The reason is that for years I have been attempting to explain to as many people as I can the magic of charity. Hut somehow, 1 feel that I failed. Everyone knows it is a good thing to do but how many know or realize it can alter the course of their destinies? Every religion, every scripture says in one way or the other: "Give... give with a pure heart and with no expectation in return, (live magnanimously. Give with love. Give to derive joy and satisfaction. And the returns shall follow you to your doorstep." And I am a living example, right before your very eyes. So, prophecies of doctors, pandits and astrologers were all proved incorrect. Babaji's blessings led Maa and Papa to a miracle called me. © So who can explain better than me, the incredible power of charity and goodness? "Give one and receive a million-fold."

My story doesn't end here. Babaji, who rarely ever left his place of stay, was so ecstatic that he actually visited nut home on the fifth day of my birth, held me in his arms and blessed me. I truly do feel like a precious child even today. It is the goodness and blessings of dear Babaji and my Maa-Papa that I am so spiritually inclined. Can never thank them enough.

So, Kambli Vaale Babaji came into our lives years before my dearest Sai Babaji. But both have taught us the same lesson... the lesson of daan (charity) and dharma (righteousness). To me, Kambli Vaale Babaji is not separate from Sai Babaji. They are both enlightened sovils, who came to this world to remind us of our inherent goodness. The power of divinity is already within us. We just need to open the big lock of greed and selfishness, throw it all out ami then goodness shall pour in and flood our lives and the lives of those around. I pray to each of you to make sure that you don't have to decide and practise charity. Make it a part of your life. Just as we breathe, eat and live each day, so also should we practise kindness and charity. And believe me, one need not have a large amount of money to carry out acts of charity. All one needs to have is a large heart. If each of us could sacrifice one meal a day or even one meal a week... millions could be fed. And the beauty of this tlivine virtue is that the more you give the more you receive. Goodness flows out and blessings flow in. So, let us give in abundance and receive in abundance too. For, even the Upanishads say, "In the Kalyug, charity shall be the noblest virtue with the greatest rewards."

Aum Sai Shrt Sai faya faya Sai

"What a man might give does not last long and it is always imperfect. But what God gives, lasts to the end of time. No other gift from any man can be compared to His. God says, cTake, take,' but everybody comes to Me and says, 'Give, give.' Nobody attends carefully to the meaning of what I say. My treasury (spiritual wealth) is full, it is overflowing. Dig out and take away this wealth in cartloads. The blessed son of a true mother should fill himself with this wealth. Body (earth) will mix with earth, bre&th with air. This time won't come again. He who carries out any spiritual endeavour will reap its fruit and he who remembers these words of Mine will get invaluable happiness."

— SAI BABA OF SHIRDI

Baba's Infinite 'Forms of Love'

"Strive not much for food and clothes. If you want anything, beg of the Lord, renounce worldly honours, try to get the Lord's grace and blessings and be honoured in His Court. Do not be deluded by worldly honour. The form of the Deity should be firmly fixed in the mind. Let all the senses and mind be ever devoted to the worship of the Lord, let there be no attraction for any other thing. Fix the mind in remembering Me always, so that it will not wander elsewhere, towards body, wealth and home. Then it will be calm, peaceful and carefree. This is the sign of the mind, being well engaged in good company. If the mind is vagrant, it cannot be called well-merged In Him."

A lot of debate has taken place over these years on Baba's birth and a lot of discussion has ensued on Baba's death as well. But I am left to wonder, what is the significance of such debates, disputes and discussions. Was He ever born that He should die?? Is God subject to birth and death? Does it really matter where He came from and where He went? Maybe to the inquisitive mind it does but to the loving heart nothing matters other than Baba's love and blessings. The truth remains that He has always been there, He is here in the 'now' and He shall be here... forever.

Baba once teasingly told His ardent devotee Shama that he had been with Baba for the last 72 births. He also once said to Dadasaheb Khaparde, who was the most affluent advocate of Amaravati and a member of the Council of State, Delhi, "I was here thousands of years ago."

Baba's words were never untrue, nor were His claims false. Several great devotees and learned men have researched and testified that Baba's words were always laden with depth and impregnated with truth.

He who could travel beyond space and time at any given moment, would He be limited by the boundaries of birth and death? Baba was known to be present at various different places, in different cities at the same time. As and when a devotee called out to Him, He appeared either in His own body or in a different roop (form), but He always did appear. It is said that Baba once sent a devotee named Balaram Mankar to a faraway city, in order to practise meditation and calm his restless mind. There, Baba appeared before Mankar in person, that too when Mankar was not in a state of meditative oneness or trance. And not only did Baba appear, He even spoke to him. AJI this while, Baba was also present in Shirdi. ☺

His ways were unique, His instructions diverse but His presence eternal-To some He appeared in dreams and aided them lovingly, to others He appeared in various forms; not only human but sometimes even as a fly, a crow, etc, and before some others He appeared as Himself, in His own body. Though the forms and methods were varied, the purpose was one... to bless and benefit His children. He is known to have appeared as a fly to partake of an offering of Puranpolis (jaggery stuffed rotis) cooked lovingly by His ardent devotee Nanasaheb Chandorkar. At another time, He appeared as a sanyasi to keep up a promise, made to one of His most learned devotees, Shri BV Dev. To some He appeared as their chosen deity and to some as their Guru. But all Baba wanted to achieve through these varied appearances and forms was a rcaffirmation of the faith of His children.

One such incident occurred in my life too and reaffirmed that what was true during Baba's lifetime is true even today. Just as He appeared in different forms to bless His children or respond to their affectionate calls back in Shirdi, He does that even today. And in this case, He fulfilled the wish of tiny Basanti, whose passionate innocence pulled Baba down to earth from His heavenly abode. ☺

Little Basanti always accompanied her mother, who worked as a helper-maid in our house. Initially, she would just sit in a corner and wait for her mother to finish her daily chores. But then, after a few days, she started insisting that she too be given some work. So, to keep her heart, my Maa told her that she could dust Baba's temple room, while she waited for her mother to get free. She was thrilled!! Though just nine years of age, she spent hours cleaning up Baba's room... a special room in our house that had been done up especially for Him. At the centre of the room was — and still is — a beautiful, medium-sized marble idol of Babaji and all around are innumerable portraits and large pictures of Babaji in different moods, unique expressions and vibrant colours. One could — arid still can — fee! bliss by merely stepping in. It feels as though Baba Himself is physically present there; one can feel His aura and light. And most of the time, we would find little Basanti taking a great deal of pain to keep even the smallest dust particle out of this room. Every Thursday (which is observed as Baba's day), His marble idol would be ritually bathed with milk, curd, honey, powdered sugar and rose water and dressed up royally. Trust me, it is so completely joyful to do so. And as this act of love was carried out week after week, we noticed that Basanti would forget all about her work and just sit in a corner and look on at Baba with pure love in her eyes.

This silent admiration of the little girl for Baba had been going on for some weeks, when 1 decided to gift her an idol of Baba, to not only increase her devotion but to also make her happy. And 1 cannot put into words how overjoyed she was to receive 'a Babaji' that she could take home with her. She asked me over and over again, "Is this idol of Baba really for me? Can I take Him home? Can I also give Him a bath every Thursday?"... and so on. ☺

Very rare and very fortunate are those people who realize their divine connect. And Basanti was surely more blessed than many others as she had realized and experienced the feeling of divine love at such a tiny age. The form of the Lord that we connect with does not matter... it could be Christ or Lord Shiva or Allah or Guru Govindji or even dear Baba. What matters is that we have unblemished faith and also an inclination towards goodness, towards divinity and towards spirituality.

So, I wanted to do all I possibly could to increase this pure feeling of love for the Lord in Basariti. I put some thought into it and after a few days, to reaffirm her devotion, 1 spoke to her tenderly, "You are a very nice girl, Basanti, and you love Baba a lot. He is very kind and always answers the honest prayers of His children. So whenever you want anything, ask Babaji for it and He will surely grant your wish."

In order to strengthen her faith in Baba's feet, I told her to ask for anything she wanted from Him right then, at that moment, in front of me; something like a nice dress or a new pair of shoes or even chocolates. I had promised myself, to get for her whatever her heart desired and gift it to her on behalf of Babafi, in order to bring a smile on her lips and make her faith deeper in her prayers and her God.

So once again I said to her, "Ask for something, Basanti. Look at Him and ask and He will surely give you whatever you desire."

She then looked at Baba very affectionately; her tiny eyes shimmering with purity and devotion, and then smiling shyly said, "I want Baba... only Baba," (Mujhe daba chahiye... sirfBaba).

I stood speechless at her expression of pure love. It was unbelievable that a poor little girl like her had not asked Baba for riches or material gifts. In fact, I realized that 1 was so wrong, so silly to have considered her poor, because outwardly her condition may have been impoverished but her inner self was so rich, so wealthy. 1 was touched and moved by her love for Baba.

For quite a while, I was at a loss for words and was only smiling in awe, but finally I spoke, "Basanti, I am really delighted to know that you want Baba but can you explain it to me with clarity how and in what form you want Him. He is already with you, in your heart. So, do you want another idol or big picture of Baba?"

1 was still looking for ways and means to satisfy her desire by gifting her yet another picture of Baba. But 1 am embarrassed to admit that I was wrong once again. Her answer cleared all my apprehensions and doubts.

"Didi, 1 want only Baba. 1 want Him and nothing else. 1 don't want His pictures, not even a dress. 1 want my Baba. Will 1 get Him?"

To be honest, 1 had no reply to her simple, innocent questions. But knowing fully well that Baba would never disregard such a pure request and would surely satisfy the little girl in one of His unique ways, 1 replied, "Yes, my dear. You will surely get Him. He will come to you. Just have faith in Him and He will not disappoint you."

Barely had a week passed by. it was a Friday morning when Basanti walked up to me. Her tiny eyes were sparkling brighter than ever before and she spoke with a shy smile and inexplicable excitement in her voice, "Didi, you were right when you said that if I have faith in Baba, He won't disappoint me."

I looked at the little girl, wondering what she was trying to convey.

She continued, "So, Didi, every day when I swept and cleaned Baba's room 1 prayed to Him that Baba, I want You, only You and finally He heard my prayers."

I kept silent, my mind flooded with thoughts and ideas as to what was coming next. I waited patiently to hear her out before I reached any conclusions.

Basanti continued, "Didi, yesterday (Thursday, Baba's day), after you finished giving a bath to Baba, I once again prayed to Him and left for home with my mother. We boarded a bus... the same bus that we take each day to get back to our place. After some time, the bus halted at a stop to pick up more passengers and, can you guess, Uiili, what happened after that?"

I fumbled, "What happened, Basanti?"

"Well, Didi," she went on, "Babaji Himself boarded the bus and came and sat down on the seat across mine."

Now this was getting too much for me to take in and T calmed myself down by assuming that little Basanti must have mistaken some elderly gentleman to be our Baba.

I lovingly smiled back at her innocence and said, "That is really nice, Basanti. I am very happy that you saw Baba."

But I was still inquisitive, "But tell me, my dear girl, what was Baba wearing? And how was He to look at?"

On hearing my query, she caught me by my hand and took me to Baba's temple room in our house. There she pointed out one of the large pictures on the wall, "He looked exactly like this picture, Didi. He was wearing a similar long white dress, had His head covered by a white patka (cloth tied around the head) and He had a beard like Babaji too."

Now I was completely puzzled and despite the fear of breaking her little heart, 1 confronted her yet again. "But, [lasanti, he may have been some other elderly man who looked like our Babaji or may be even a sage or sadhti dressed up like Him. How are you so sure that he was our Sai Baba?"

To this she flashed a huge confident smile at me, "Oh, Didi, He was none other than my Babaji because even in the bus, He sat with His right leg crossed on His left knee and even His left hand was on the same foot as it is in His pictures." (To those who know about Babaji, this indication is huge, because Baba is known to have always sat in this posture when He was alive. What surprised me though, was how a girl as young as Basanti had observed and correlated this fact without knowing the details.)

She continued excitedly, "And you know, Ditll, all along the way He kept looking at me and smiling. But the smile was not new. 1 immediately recognized it because every day Baba gives me the same smile from His picture too. So He was my Sal Baba and no one else."

I stood frozen to the spot, my heart palpitating loud enough for Basanti to hear. "We did not speak to each other, Dktl," she went on, "but when He got up at another stop to gel off the bus, He smiled at me and blessed me by keeping His hand on my head and then walked away. So, 1 am very happy. And now 1 know for sure that whenever I want to meet Him again, He will surely come."

Now I leave it to the readers to Imagine what were my feelings when I heard this incredible experience of little Basanti. The shine in Basanti's eyes and the innocent confidence on her face told my heart that each word she spoke was true. I thought I was being very intelligent and mature when 1 tried to strengthen her faith, by asking her to pray to Baba for any heartfelt wish. But the supposedly immature and naive nine-year-old girl had instead ended up strengthening my faith and giving me a bigger lesson in return.... If one calls out to Baba with faith. He not only fulfils our wishes by sending us gifts and blessings from His abode but even steps down Himself, if our prayers are sincere and pure.

Baba, as we all know, runs to His devotees whenever and wherever they call out to Him with love. Then what can one say about the love of a pure-hearted child to which one can draw no possible comparisons. So Baba Himself walked up to Basanti, to fulfil an honest wish and to bless His tittle daughter. 1 had not witnessed what Basanti had, but my heart wanted to believe every word... I could see the verity and joy in her little eyes. He never lets down His children.

I'd like to repeat here the sacred words, **"As men believe in Me, so do 1 accept them". So, in whatever form and with whatever feeling we call out to Him, in the very same form, He manifests Himself before us, to satisfy our heart's deepest desires... the deeper our love, the stronger our faith, the faster Baba's response.** Please, Baba, accept our prayers, the prayers of all Your children, as we come together in sending a special message across to You, **"We love You, Babaji, and WE ALSO WANT ONLY YOU."** ☺

Aum Sai Shri Sai Jaya)aya Sai

"Those who resort to this Masjid shall never suffer anything in this life to the end of time. Now, do not worry. Apply Udi on the point of the disease a-nd the diseased shall recover. Relieve in God! This is no Masjid, but Dwark&mai. He, who steps here, will soon get health and happiness and his sufferings will come to an end."

— SAI BABA OF SHIRDI

Udi is Baba and Baba is Udi

Baba taught by His Vdi that all the visible phenomena In the universe are as transient as the ash. Our bodies, composed of matter of the five elements, will fall down after all their enjoyments are over and be reduced to ashes. Baba also taught by the Vdi that Brahma is the only Reality and the universe is ephemeral and that no one in this world, be he a son, father or wife, is really ours. We come here (tit this world) alone and we have to go from here alone.

The teelas of dear Baba are unfathomable. The deeper a devotee delves, the more intensely does he get soaked in His divine love. Baba took samadhi on 15 October, 1918, and left His mortal coil. His hfmktas could no longer touch Him or see His physical form and were extremely saddened by Baba's passing away. Rut the kind and merciful Baba, as a sign of His remembrance, left for His bhaktas the precious and sacred 'Udi'. Also known commonly among His bhaktas as 'Vibhuti', this was Baba's greatest gift to humanity. Even as He left the material world, He was deeply concerned about our well-being and happiness. So He blessed us, His children, with the Udi, which is nothing else but Baba personified. This Vibhuti embodies Baba's soul. Though Baba took samadiii and became tine with the Universal Soul, He stayed back in this world, in the tactile form as well. This form of Baba, better known a;, His Udi is forever alive with His Divine 1'resence. He lives as The Sacred Udi' even today, for the welfare of His children. Those who have been fortunate enough to realize this presence have benefited immensely. Here is the true experience of a devout bhukta for whom Baba's Udi was verily Baba Himself.

This beautiful leela is about Hajan I'urohit, a devotee of Baba. I met him through a friend and so warm and affectionate was his disposition that I took an immediate (iking to him and started addressing him as Rajan Bhaiya (elder brother). If one was to meet him, one would definitely smile at the way he could endlessly talk about his Sai. He shares a very special relation with Baba. He fights with Baba, shouts at Him, even calls Him budha (old man) but loves Baba beyond imagination. He visits Shirdi 12 times a year... © WOW!! Amazing devotion!

Rajan Btwiya had a very sweet baby boy named Karthik, who was just learning to take his first steps; a tiny life that had illumined his world. Bhaiya told me with a twinkle in his eyes, "Time would fly by, thanks to my love, my Karthik. The day's fatigue and stress would disappear at his first welcoming smile. He was and is Baba's biggest blessing in our life."

Then dawned a morning, which was destined to be the beginning of trials, tests and tribulations for the whole family. All of a sudden, iittle Karthik could no more take those baby steps. In fact, he could no longer even stand on his tiny feet. One fateful day, this 1W-year-old baby was diagnosed with a disease called rickets. The joints of his tiny feet got affected and this resulted in his feet turning inwards. All the celebrations of the baby's first steps transformed overnight into gloom and sadness.

A couple of years passed by but the disease only worsened. Rajan Bhaiya consulted every possible doctor but in vain. Medical treatment was not helping little Karthik at all. Desperate attempts at reviving the baby boy's joints were failing and helplessness was looming large. The worst blow came finally when doctors informed the parents that they did not anticipate any chances of the baby getting cured. He would probably never, ever walk. The disease had affected his bones at a very tiny age; there was no hope. This news left the family distraught and shattered. Till then at least their hope was keeping them alive and going but the final verdict from several distinguished doctors snatched away that ray of hope and that, too, mercilessly. Only the wearer knows where the shoe bites and in this case those that have experienced the suffering or pain of holding a little baby helplessly in their arms can truly empathize with such grief-

stricken parents.
But, doctors are doctors and lijitui is Huba. He is 'light', He is 'positivity', He is 'hope'.... And our dear Uajiin Hlmiyn may have been momentarily disillusioned by the verdict at the doctors, hut his faith in Baba was as strong as ever. He told me, while narratins this Incident, "I told the budha, 'I will not leave You, come what may. You better take care of my baby. Else I will not spare You. 1 am warning You; there is no option available to You other than curing my Karthik.'"

Strange is the love of Baba's children. © Some cry before Him, some beg, some fight with Him and some others even threaten. This happens because to some He is a Father, to some a Friend, to some a Brother and to some a Guru. But to all of us, He is our God, our Lord, our Soul, our courage, our inner strength, our willpower... our everything.

Time passed by, Karthik was now four years. His condition had grown from bad to worse. The disease was now impacting more than just the joints of his feet and was raring to spread throughout his little body. Rajan Bhaiya could no longer bear the pain and trauma of seeing his baby suffer and, so, with a heart as heavy as a mountain, he decided to visit Shirdi. There, he cried his heart out to Baba at the Samadhi Mandir and prayed for showers of mercy.

"I will not go anywhere, Baba, till You bless Karthik and show me the way to cure him. Tell me, Baba, what should I do, where should I go? If You my Father cannot help me, it is better that 1 die. I would any day prefer death over seeing my baby suffer and die. Take my life, Baba, but give a healthy, happy Karthik back to me. please, Baba!!"

And we all know how soft our sweetheart Baba's heart is. Our tears are like fire for Baba's heart... they bring it to melting point in seconds. Rajan Bbaiya's tears were no exception. So dear Baba showed him the path away from darkness and towards light.... Like I said before, Baba may come to us in any form, any roo/j; it may be human or may be just a powerful thought. That same evening, as Rajan Bhaiya sat praying in Baba's Dwarkamai, facing Baba's ever-burning Dhani, it was, as though, Baba blessed him with an instant solution to his troubles and miseries... the infallible remedy... the Sacred Ashes of the Dhuni... Baba's Udi. Baba lit a lamp within Rajan Bhaiya and transformed his weakness into his strength. His helplessness reinforced into utmost faith and Rajan Bhaiya took back with him a box hill of Udi from Baba's Dhuni at Dwarkamai. So strong was his faith in Baba that against the wishes of his parents and his wife, he completely stopped all of Karthik's medication. The family fought with him and he fought back adamantly.

"No!! Karthik will not be given any medication, come what may!!"

Each night he would apply handfuls of Udi all over Karthik's tiny body, pray to Sai to cure him and put him to sleep. This routine went on day after day.

Fifteen days had gone by. One bright, beautiful morning, when Karthik's mother went running to his early morning cries, she screamed loud enough for the bricks in the walls to fall over. Rajan Khaiya and others rushed to the room, only to see Karthik standing by the bedside, smiling. His feet were firm on the ground like any other healthy baby and he looked bright and salubrious. There was no sign of the disease, no traces and no side effects. Karthik was in the pink of health and doctors were green and blue in disbelief at the failure of science against the strength of faith. Baba's '/anclii udi' (that's what I call it) had once again shown its magic. Sai was smiling from up above and Karthik's family was bowing at His feet in gratitude and joy. 'Faith works wonders that even prayers can't... because even prayers are worked by faith/ So keep your faith firm and your patience unwavering.

Baba's Udi is His special endowment to His children, His bequest of love. It is a priceless legacy that Baba's children have inherited from Him... the Father.

As a rule, all His children must apply Udi to their foreheads

after a bath, when leaving the house for work or at the time of starting out on a new venture or task. They must also begin their day by having a pinch of Udi mixed in a little water, first thing in the morning and end their day by drinking the nectar of Udi last thing at night. Anyone who is unwell or diseased must be given Udi mixed in water along with a sincere prayer to Baba to rid him/her of the ailment. Have faith in Baba's Udi, believing it to be Baba Himself and He will free you from all material, physical and temporal difficulties and flood your present as well as your future with light and energy.

Aum Sai Shri Sai Jaya Jaya Sai

"There will never be any dearth or scarcity, regarding food and clothes, in My devotees' homes. It is My special characteristic that I always look after and provide for the welfare of those devotees, who worship Me wholeheartedly with their minds ever fixed on Me."

— SAI BABA OF SHIRDI

The Magic of Baba's Udi: Replicated and Retold

"When the devotees surrender themselves completely to Me, I see to it that the religious functions in their houses are duly executed and complied with all the necessary formalities."

His eyes were, are and shall remain the 'Eyes of God'. One look endears Him to all. One glance cures the deadliest diseases. One eye-to-eye, heart-to-heart 'connect' and the gross body ceases to exist. We lose all identification to our name, our form, our bodily existence. All that remains is Oneness... Divine Sublime Oneness; such is our Sai, our Baba... our love.

Baba's endowment, His Udi, is multifunctional, multi-purpose and multi-magical. © When someone is suffering from a disease, it manifests as medicine; when someone is lacking courage, it manifests as inner strength; when someone is hungry, it manifests as food; when someone is failing, it manifests as success; when someone is disillusioned, it manifests as a solution; when anything is scarce, it obliterates the scarcity.... It is truly magical, .surreal and mesmerizing. It takes any shape, any form, any name, any time, anyhow, to help the devotee in need or distress... just like dear Baba.

Time and again, I smile in bewilderment... It feels as though Baba is bringing some pictures, some incidents before me like flashbacks of older times; times that I have not experienced in this life, but times which are more than real anci resounding in my memories, thanks to Baba's Satcharita. Yes, I envision repeat telecasts of Baba's lifetimes in Shirdi. What happened back then, reoccurs, reappears and resonates before my eyes, over and over again. The characters of the play have changed; Baba, who was then present in the body, is now present as the Soul... but the exact incident replicates after almost hundred years.

I have many such stories to be retold, many such instances to be recapped. 1 don't want to miss even a single one, as each incident reaffirms our faith that Baba, who was alive a hundred years back, is as alive even today. Nothing, absolutely nothing has changed. Even then He was an honest prayer away, and even today He is an honest prayer away.

Sharing the first one that comes to my mind...

It was 11 April, 2003, and we — my family and I — were all excited and happily engaged in making grand preparations for the evening. A Bha/an Sandhya (singing hymns and devotional songs) in praise of Baba was being organized to mark the celebration of the auspicious Ram Navami festival (Lord Rani's birthday). It was a very special day for us, too, as these celebrations were also being carried out to seek His blessings, for a new house that we had purchased recently. A large number of people had been invited and the bhajan was to be followed by Baba's Bhog Prasad as dinner.

The bhajan finally commenced with a prayer to Lord Ganesha and was followed by Baba's divine rhythms and songs of adulation and love. Baba's durbar looked imposing. There were innumerable pictures and idols adorning the main hall. Incense sticks, lights, lamps and divatyas made the ambience celestial. The evening was overflowing with His grace. Melodious bhajans flooded the atmosphere and stirred the hearts of one and all. Some cried, some laughed, some sang, some danced... all the devotees were in a state of trance and were deeply absorbed in the vibrations of Baba's mellifluous songs of devotion and love. We could actually feel Baba's presence amongst us. It felt as if we had risen from the earth and reached Baba's heavenly abode.

All good things come to an end. After an ecstatic evening spent in celebrating His name, this blissful evening too came to its end and culminated into the night, with the aarti ceremony being performed. Baba was then offered the bhog with loads of affection and, after consecrating the food in this manner, preparations were made to serve dinner. On such devotional dinner evenings, the norm is that Baba is first offered the prepared meals and sweets, and then the food, thus offered, is mixed with the main dish, which is now served as holy prasad to all those present.

We seated all our guests for the consecrated dinner and stalled serving. It was then that my parents realized that almost twice the number of guests expected had turned up and the food would just not suffice for everyone present. This ushered a feeling of panic and helplessness. The whole family was in a state of anxiety and shuddered at the fear of embarrassment and the dishonour that would come to the family. It would amount to complete disgrace, if the devotees gathered had to be refused food. People had just commenced eating and the dishes were close to empty, with no more food to replenish them.

But we are Baba's children; we couldn't panic for too long. After all it was Baba's evening, Baba's bhog. It was His responsibility to uphold the dignity of the family. So we turned to Baba in this hour of crisis. While our parents continued to serve whatever little was available, my sister and I rushed to Baba's imposing durbar and pleaded before Him to show us the way. "Guide us, Baba, what should we do? Devotees are still eating and we have no food to serve and no time to organize some more. Please show us the way, Baba. Please!!"

As we stood before Baba, praying, suddenly a thought flashed through my mind. It was as though Baba had walked into my head and put the answer there, i recalled a miracle of our dear Baba that I had read in the Sliri Sai Satcharita several times. A similar situation of shortage of food had once arisen in the house of Balaji Patil Newaskar, a devotee of Baba. Each time I think of him, my heart is filled with respect and admiration. His love for Baba was so deep and so pure that when he reaped his corn each year, he carried the entire harvest to Baba and offered it at His feet. Out of that, whatever Baba returned with love, in that Balaji sustained himself and his family. And this continued year after year and after Balaji's death, even his son kept up the tradition. What kind of detached, divine love is this?? i can only pay my respects to such devotees, whose love for Baba is far above any material objects oc attachments.

Once, on Balaji's death anniversary a large number of people were invited for prayers and meals. Far more than the expected number of guests turned up. Balaji's wife had complete faith in her Baba Sai. She prayed to Baba to save the family from ignominy and maintain their respect. Then on the suggestion of her mother-in-law, with unwavering faith in Baba, Balaji's wife added His Udi to all the dishes and covered them with a piece of cloth and then kept serving from these covered dishes. And magic happened!! With Baba's grace, no one returned without food and all were fed to their heart's content.

When this incident flashed through my mind, we too immediately decided to do the same. Baba is so close to all our hearts that we knew He would surely come to our rescue and never ever let us down. How can there ever be a shortage of Baba's prasadl So with unflinching faith in Him, we added the Sacred Udi to all the dishes in the pantry, covered these with a cloth and started refilling the service dishes from there. And behold the grace of our Sai! Not only were all the guests fed with the sumptuous and wholesome food but lots of it was left over too! © We actually had to pack the remaining prasad and give, it to the people to take home. It was unbelievable that the dishes remained ever-full despite the fact that over a hundred extra guests had been fed, in addition to those expected. 1 recall vividly, even to this day, how everyone complimented the delectably cooked food, ate beyond their capacity and still there was no end to the food in our serving dishes. Who else but Baba could have replenished those empty dishes and blessed us with this miracle of love and faith?

Baba's Udi, His miraculous Sacred Ashes, are a gift of His

unconditional love to His children. 1 challenge anyone in this world to prove me wrong, as I commit, under oath, that there is no task that cannot be accomplished, no pain that cannot be relieved, no wish that cannot be realized if we have faith in Baba and His Udi. Anyone, who begins the day by partaking a little Udi mixed in water and ends the day with the same, is wrapped in divine energy and light, which may not be visible to the human eye, but shall surely be visible in their lives.

Sai always helps His children in moments of crisis. He cares for us, the way no one else does. He is seated in our heart and knows our innermost thoughts and concerns. Whenever we are confronted by a problem, however big, He brings the situation under control. How could He then have let us down or sent back His children without being fed? So He gave us in abundance, not only His pra.iad but also His boundless love. **We pray unto Your Divine Feet, Baba, please never forsake us. If we go wrong, correct us but never abandon us because You are the beam of sunshine in our lives. Please love us as Your own and keep us safely inside Your effulgent heart.**

Aum Sai Shri Sai Jaya Jaya Sai

"I never know, when I am angry with My children. If it is possible that mothers could kick their children and the sea turn back the rivers, I too could neglect My devotees' welfare. I, the Slave of My devotees, always stand by them and respond to them., whenever they call upon Me. And I always long for their love."

— SAI BABA OF SHIRDI

Maa, Blessing I: When Fire could not Burn

The efficacy of find's name is well known. It saves us from all sins and bad tendencies, frees us from the cycle of births and deaths. There is no easier Sadhana than this. It is the best purifier of our mind. It requires no paraphernalia and no restrictions. It is so easy and so effective.

Baba could easily command Mother Nature and communicate with her. Both flora and fauna not only understood Baba's language but also instantly conceded to His orders. Once there was a devastating storm in Shirdi. The clouds thundered mercilessly and poured down in torrents, Shirdi was completely flooded and the residents were extremely terrified. They rushed to Baba and sought His refuge,

Baba, who loved His children dearly, came out of His Uwarkamai and shouted aloud in a powerful voice, at the thundering clouds, "Stop, stop your fury and be calm." And within minutes, peace and calm embraced Shirdi. The rains stopped and the tempest disappeared.

On another day, the flames in Baba's Dhuiii were rising higher and higher, unabated, and almost reached the roof of the masjid. When Baba observed this, He merely hit His satka (short stick) against a pillar and ordered the flames to tool down. "Get down, be calm."

Each time His stick struck the pillar, the flames receded. He needed no water; His words were enough to subdue the rising, infuriated flames.

At another time, Shama — a devotee who was especially close lo

Baba's heart — was bitten by a snake on his little finger and the poison began to spread through his body. He thought that he was nearing his end and rushed to seek Baba's blessings in the masjifl.

On seeing him, Baba screamed angrily, "Go, get way, come down!"

As Shama later realized, it was not an order to him but to the poison, not to rise up in the body and to disappear along with its ill effects. As commanded by Baba, the poison stopped spreading and soon Shama felt better.

So one can very well see that Sai could speak to nature, plants and animals and even they immediately responded to His authoritative words.

Here is a similar teeta of Sai that will leave you spellbound. My Maa is a very pious lady; very simple and pure at heart, and Baba loves simplicity and purity more than any other virtue. He Himself lived a iife of complete simplicity. His devotees wanted to keep Him like a king, but He preferred tn live like a poor fakir... such was His plainness. Though Baba received thousands of rupees as dakshina during His lifetime, He distributed the entire amount to His devotees and possessed almost nothing on His person, when He left this world. His only belongings included a tin-pot, a rectangular bag made of cloth, a short stick and an earthen smoking pipe. He was content wearing an old torn kafni (long dress), while His devotees wanted to dress Him up in robes, jewels and crowns, Baba was very plain and straightforward... a simple, holy soul... not only in all outward appearances but also internally. And so it is not surprising that He has a special place in His heart for pure-hearted, humble and unpretentious devotees. And 1 am sure that is why He loves my Maa so much.

This dates back to a time when I was in my twenties. Early one morning, Maa woke up and went into the kitchen. My dad, my sister and I were all still asleep. She lit up the gas stove, to prepare tea for ail of us and placed a pan on it. While she was waiting for the water to boil, she went to Baba's temple room and, tike every other day, she woke Him up affectionately (His idol) and prayed to Him to always be by her side. It was and is always her routine to wake Baba up with loads of affection. Sometimes when I see her next to Baba, she appears like His mother too. ☺ On that day as well, after smothering Baba's forehead with kisses, she came back to prepare tea. The water had not started boiling yet. As she was waiting, she noticed a huge, dirty utensil used for boiling milk lying in the basin. It was empty and dry. While she waited, she filled it with water up to the brim. As she turned to prepare tea, she observed something strange behind her. Before she could realize what it was, she felt a surge of heat on her back. As she looked behind her shoulder, she was stunned. Her clothes had caught fire and the flames were rising from her legs right up to her shoulders. The heat was too much to bear.

OUT bedroom was a little too far. Neither could Maa have reached us in time to be saved by us, nor could her screams. By the time we would have woken up and grasped how critical the situation was, it would have been too late. Realizing this, our brave Maa — a lady with great presence of mind — did not shout aloud for us but called out to her Sai instead, "Save me, L>?va, please save me,"

It was all very momentary and happened within seconds. Repeating "Sai Ram, Sai Ram" amidst the entire panic and the flames, she turned around towards Sai's beautiful picture up on the side wall of the kitchen, and the very next thing that caught her eye was the huge vessel full of water that she had just filled. It was a message... she suddenly felt strength rush through her veins. By now she was in flames!! She immediately picked up the huge container full of water and taking Baha's name poured it on herself. The fire subsided a little but her dupatta (scarf) was still in flames. As she pulled it away from her body, it got stuck in her neck and the fire was now on her face. She still managed to throw it away and now that the fire had lessened in intensity, she ran and woke us up.

Dad ran out of his room and my sister Neha and I rushed out of the other. We were horrified at the sight. Maa did not have even a small strip of cloth on her entire back side. On the floor were burnt, ash-like remainders of her dress. The flames had completely destroyed her clothes. One can well imagine how badly scalded and scorched her back would be.

As we ran towards Maa in panic, to check how bad her burns were, we were in for the most unbelievable sight. As impossible as it may sound, Maa's back did not even have a tiny scar, forget about the bums. It still leaves me awestruck, when I try to cognize how this could have happened; huge flames of fire burn away every strand of cloth on your body, yet the body remains untouched by the fire! It appeared as though her Deva had rushed to her rescue and had ordered the fire, "Don't burn." ☺

But Maa's chin was real bad. Though she had pulled off the dupatta from her neck, a portion had got stuck to her chin. So when we saw Maa, her chin still had fire within. It was visibly burning. The remnant cloth of her dupatta was still ablaze and so was her chin. Dad rushed and poured some water over it. At this time, Maa was screaming aloud in agony. The flesh was all gone and the pink, moist inner layer was now strikingly visible and was unbearably painful. We didn't know what first aid to give to such a deep burn.

In obvious panic, while Dad and I were still contemplating what to do next, Neha immediately picked up the little box of Udi that is a permanent item on our dining table. With tears in her eyes and with constant chanting of Baba's name, "Sai Ram, Sai Ram," she took a handful of Udi out of it and slowly sprinkled it on Maa's bum from a little distance. Even before she had finished sprinkling the Udi completely, Maa stopped crying and appeared calmer and relaxed.

Though shaken by the whole traumatic incident, she smiled at us, "My Deva saved me. And He has taken away the pain as well. I am all right. Please don't worry."

Another miracle of Baba had happened within moments. ☺ The pain had completely died out.

Dad did consult a doctoi who refused to believe that alt her clothes were burnt to ashes and there was not even the smallest visible scraping or scarring on her entire back. He suggested an ointment for the burn on her chin, which Maa never used. By applying the Udi regularly and by drinking it mixed in a little water, Maa recovered fully and even the marks disappeared over a period of time.

Words fail me as I try to explain the sentiments of my family, especially those of Maa. First Baba got the vessel of water filled up, right on time to save her, then the fire burnt her clothes to ashes but could not even touch her and finally the single painful burn was absolutely cured by applying Baba's Sacred Udi. Such is our Sai... the epitome of mercy and compassion. Had Maa rushed to us, we may not have been able to save her. But anyone who calls out Father Sai's all-purifying name can never be unaided and is sure to be saved. In the biggest of challenges and trials, he who remembers Baba with love and faith, gets a definitive response.

When Baba was alive and in His physical form, He had once pushed His arm into the scorching hot fire of His Dhtmi at Dwarkamai, in order to save a little baby who had slipped off its mother's lap, into a furnace, in same distant village. Baba's arm was charred completely but little did He care about the deep burns. He was still all smiles that the little baby could be saved. Baba did not permit any doctor to touch His arm, forget even examining it. His devotees pleaded, called the famous physician Dr Parmanantl, from Bombay (now Mumhai) but Baba did not concede to any request. His leper devotee Bhagoji Shinde massaged the arm with ghee, then placed a leaf on it and bandaged it tightly, every day, till Baba's Maiiasamadlii. How can we ever doubt the love of such a benevolent God as Baba?

He cares for us like no one else. **Family, friends and all worldly relationships are limited by our breaths and heart beats. But**

our relationship with Baba has been there for uncountable births. He was always with us, is always with us and shall always remain with us. He is our only permanent relation. How can He ever forsake us or leave us suffering? Trust Him with all you have and life will be blissful.

Almost a hundred years ago, He saved the little baby and now He came to the rescue of Maa. He is the Almighty Father of the Universe. He is the life of nature, the essence of love. He is the only one, who can command fire by mere words, "Fire! Do not burn!!"☺

There is no end to Baba's mercies and kindness. The more 1 thank Him, the lesser I feel it is. Can we ever thank the sun enough for giving us sunshine day after day? Or can we ever thank the moon and the stars for lighting up the darkness of our nights? Then how, just how can we thank dear Baba enough? He who floods our lives with His love, He who exhilarates our souls with His warmth, He who illumines our world with His light... His grace is endless, our vocabulary limited. All we can do is love Him with the same obsessive passion with which He loves us. The words 'obsessive passion' may sound out of place when referring to God, but the fact is that **Baba hungers for our love just as we hunger for His. The more our obsessive passion for Baba, the more the madness in our love for Him and the more the madness in our love, the deeper our 'connect' with Baba.**

Maa, Blessing II: Baba - The Wirepuller of the Show of the Universe

I must share another grace of Baba in my mother's life. As I have mentioned earlier, her love for Baba is unique; she calls Him Deva affectionately. During the winter months I have seen her covering Baba with a warm shawl, cosying up Baba with her warm embraces and in the summers, refilling cold water for Him and wiping His forehead (of His idol ©) with a soft wet towel, as though Baba is sweating in the heat! She sings to Him when she feeds Him, wakes Him up or puts Him to sleep and yes, she has innovated some songs of love that only she and her Deva comprehend and also delight in. When she is in a problem, He becomes her Father and at all other times He appears more tike her Son. Unparalleled and inimitable is her love for Baba. There is surely an obsessive madness to it. ☺

Maa was once diagnosed with a cyst (a lump of mass) in her inner knee. The growth was huge and caused her unbearable pain and discomfort. She could neither walk nor sit comfortably due to the huge mass. We were all really concerned and consulted various doctors. Several tests were carried out and the doctors advised that a surgery was inevitable; however, before any surgical procedure could be carried out, it was important to test the growth as it unfortunately appeared malignant. Most doctors were of the opinion that such growths could be cancerous and certainly needed immediate examination. On the basis of the tests carried out till then, they suggested thai she must be operated upon and stay in the hospital for observation for at least 10-15 days. My sister Neiia, who was at this time pregnant, lived in a different city due to her husband's transferable job. It was her first baby and due to certain health concerns, doctors had advised that she should in no case be subjected to any kind of stress or tension. So we were all extremely worried about Maa and also about the impact Maa's news could have on her.

Let me share now the bigger reason for our concern: my maternal grandmother had been diagnosed with cancer at a very young age, had suffered immensely and passed away when she was only 47. And several doctors had informed us that cancer can be genetic. If this disease has occurred previously in the family, it may occur again. So that was truly a huge cause for our anxiety. In addition, some family friend had visited our home a few months back, along with an astrologer. I must mention here that as a family, we never went to astrologers in our entire life. For us, Baba's presence was more than we could ask for; but this particular astrologer was forced upon us. We didn't want to consult him but by virtue of sitting in our living room, with our family friend, he had not .spared us from his sermons and predictions. None of us showed him our palms but our simple mother, who has still not learnt to say 'no', sat down next to him, to keep his respect as he was a guest in our house.

How much ever I hate to say this, but after looking at Maa's palm, he immediately said, "Oh!! A major calamity is to befall you at the age of 65. It will be a health issue that you will most likely not survive."

I wanted to throw the man down from the balcony of our house! Is that the way to talk or predict? But I can't deny it; he instilled a fear of the unknown in our hearts. And just to share my fears with you, when Maa was diagnosed with the lump, she was 65.

Let me narrate here an incident from the time when Baba was living in Shirdi. Back then, a young boy named Babu Tendulkar had to appear for his medical exam. He consulted astrologers, who told him that his luck was unfavourable and he should only appear for the exam the next year, as this year he would not qualify. His mother, Mrs Savitribai

Tendulkar, the author of Shri Sainatli Rhajan Mala, a beautiful book on Baba, visited Shirdi and informed Baba about her son's depressive state. At this, **Baba said, "Tell your son to believe in Me, to throw aside horoscopes and predictions of astrologers and palmists and go on with his studies. Tell him to appear for the examination with a calm mind, he is sure to pass this year. Ask him to trust in Me and not to get disappointed."**

Babu loved Baba dearly; his Baba could never be wrong. Setting aside all worries and doubts, he worked even harder than before and, true to Baba's words, he cleared the examination in that very same year. **Astrologers can surely predict the future but Baba who is our God can change it and give it a new direction...** then why fear horoscopes, when Baba's grace is shining on us? Baba's children are so strong within that they do not need the external props of predictions and prophecies to live their lives. To us, Baba's word is the final decree and there is nothing beyond it.

So, back to the story of my life... while the doctors did their work, we did ours. We prayed and prayed and prayed endlessly. My Papa is a very pious, spiritual person. In fact, I owe my own spirituality and inner growth to him. He has the calmest disposition ever, nothing invigorates him and nothing wearies him. 1 have learnt so much by merely being in his presence. These days, he was meditating every day before Baba and also reading Baba's Satcharita and praying that Maa's growth should not be cancerous. Maa, too, was religiously applying Udi to her growth and drinking the Udi mixture morning and evening with complete faith in Baba. We didn't inform Neha about the complications or the fear of malignancy but from whatever little she knew, she too prayed with utmost faith in Baba and so did her husband Uaurav. She was at this time, doing a Chatisa of Baba (reading and completing the Sai Satcharita in forty days) for her baby-to-come. And she was also praying for Maa's health throughout her Cltalisa.

I prayed, meditated, begged and beseeched Baba for His blessings. 1

told Him, "Raba, if anything happens to Maa, who will sing for You, pamper You and feed You? We call You Sai Maa. Who knows a mother's importance better than You, our Universal Mother? Bless her, please."

I visited Baba's temple and promised to come back along with Maa and offer Him His favourite, the delicious Motichur Laddoos (a type of mitllai), and urged that there should be no complication, no cancerous growth and no requirement for a surgery for Maa. My husband, who is very attached to her, also promised Baba that He would bring Maa and Papa to Shirdi to thank Him personally, if all went well.

We were eventually referred to a very senior surgeon who was to carry out the final few tests and investigations and admit Maa in the hospital for surgery. Still praying, we reached the hospital and met the doctor with all her reports. After looking through all her papers, he checked Maa's growth and carried out a very detailed examination. 1 could almost hear my heart pounding and tears welling up in my eyes, as Papa, Maa and I waited patiently for the doctor's final verdict.

He finally looked up from his papers and spoke, "There is absolutely nothing to be concerned about. The growth is not malignant or cancerous and is in fact completely harmless. I am surprised at her papers and reports. All old reports indicate towards a cancerous growth and strangely the latest ones arc absolutely clear. There is no need for a surgery; she only needs to be put on light medication for a few days and she'll be fine. Nor is there any need to admit her in hospital. You can take her back home without any fear or anxiety."

God!! I almost thought it was Baba and no! the doctor who spoke. We were ecstatic! After consulting over ten different doctors, who all shared negative opinions about Maa and her reports, here we were with clear reports and positive results. It was nothing but pure magic... Sai's magic. He so beautifully pulls the strings that even before we can realize, everything falls in place. He heard our prayers and saved Maa once again. And soon we were all at Shirdi, thanking

Baba and celebrating His love. ☺

A pure, simple heart, unswerving faith and unending patience are all you need and no trouble, however big, can ever touch you, because Mother Sai, will make even the biggest mountain of problems seem like a small, unimposing ant-hill. So love Him, trust Him and chant His name witb every breath; let every drop of your existence be flooded with His Supreme All-purifying Name and live a stress-free, trouble-free peaceful life... a life blessed by Mother Sai.

Aum Sai Shri Sai Jayu Jaya Sai

Shama, after saluting Baba said, "Deva, what is this play of Tours'? Tou first raise a storm and make us restless and then calm it down and comfort us." Baba replied, "You see, mysterious is the path of action. Though I do nothing, they hold Me responsible for the actions which take place on account o/ Prarabdha [destiny]. I am only their witness. The Lord is the sole Doer and Jnspirer. He is most merciful. Neither I am God nor Master. I am His obedient servant and remember Him constantly. He, who casts aside his egoism and thanks Him and he, who trusts Him entirely, will have his shackles removed and will obtain liberation."

— SAI BABA OF SHIRDI

Rishi, Blessing I: Baba's Miracle Child

"Wealth and prosperity are transient and the body is subject to death and decay. Knowing thin, do your duty, leaving aside all attachment to the things of this world and the next. He who does this and surrenders himself to the Feet of Hari (Lord) will get free from all troubles and attain Miss."

I look into His eyes and 1 am flooded with a euphoric outburst of love... a love exclusive to the children of Baba. The body melts into thin air and a soul craving to merge into Him remains. I can't help but wonder how people, who met Baba in person, must have lived through those moments. When looking at Baba's idol can take my breath away, I am left to marvel what exhilaration those fortunate, blessed devotees must have experienced, who looked into those divine eyes. No wonder, each description of when they first saw Baba, narrates the tales of their exuberance. Some said they wanted to roll in the dust of Baba's feet, some others said they felt cleansed of all karmic bondages, while some said that the whole world appeared to merge into Baba. The beauty of seeing Baba is that each one testified to an experience of bliss supreme.

In his diary, Dadasaheb Khaparde says, "Sayin* Sahib spoke with such a wonderful sweetness and he smiled so often and wilh such extraordinary grace that those conversations will remain engraved in my memory."

Supremely fortunate were those who saw Baba smiling those nourishing, reassuring and captivating smiles. Bless their souls. ☺

Baba healed many — all those suffering from fatal, deadly diseases — by merely smiling those 'magnetic' smiles. He could pull out terminal

*Dadasaheb addressed Sai as Sayin

"Dadasaheb addressed Sal as 5ayin ailments at will, by a mere glance at the patient or by a word of blessing. A young boy, who suffered from the incurable, tubercular bone abscess and had no hope of life, was completely healed by Baba's affectionate, warm glances and by the application of His all-powerful Udi. Such was His Grace. Our Baba, a great Sicictha, a doctor of doctors, needed no medication to treat His children. His love was the most potent, invincible medicine. Uncountable people were benefitted. Various findings testify to the fact that Baba would pull out the devotee's ailment and take it upon Himself, regardless of the pain that He would suffer in the bargain. Once a devotee, Mrs RA Tarkhad, came with painful, watering eyes and sat before Baba. Baba looked at her affectionately and smiled. Within a few moments her eyes ceased to water, the pain disappeared and to her utter disbelief, dear Baba's eyes started watering instead. Such was His love for His children.

Yet another devotee, Dr Pilley, suffered from excruciating pain due to the presence of guinea worms in his leg. He sent a message to Baba that he would prefer death over such pain.

"I know this must be a payback of my old karmas," he said. "Request my Baba to transfer this karmic settlement to ten future births of mine, so that I don't have to suffer so much pain at one go."

To this, the kind Baba replied, "Bring him here on somebody's back. In ten days, we can work out his karmic debts and sufferings. When i am here to give him temporal and spiritual welfare, why will he suffer for ten births?"

And true to His word, Baba cured him in the next ten minutes and in the next ten days Dr Pilley recovered completely. ☺

Such was His power. He was none other than the Lord God Himself. I have heard so many stories of Baba in the long years of knowing Him. Every story has been unique, every experience breathtaking. But this one miracle of Baba's love that I am joining to share, is guaranteed to leave you breathless and tearful; it is very close to my heart and so is the angel, about whom it is. Yes!! This incident relates to a young, handsome, 18-year-old boy, Rishank Chibbar, better known as Rishi — a prodigy at studies, a sensation in sports, vivacious and abounding with life.

It all happened on 29 May, 2003. Rishi, who was a student of DPS Noida, had topped in his Class XII boards and it was a day of celebration and festivity for his whole family. Everyone was rejoicing and revelling in the moment. Big plans were being made for Rishi's bright future. He was now, all set, to take the law entrance and then make his career as a flourishing lawyer. But we human beings propose one thing, while life proposes another. Seasons change, people change and so do the colours of our life. Similar is Rishi's story... from colour to black and white and then...?? You'll know at the end of this story.

It is so difficult to pen down this life-shaking incident of Rishi's life... my life. The strange thing is that where this story begins, Rishi is unknown in my life and where it ends, Rishi is my life. Mystifying are the ways of Sai. Unknown people cross paths and one day they make paths for each other. By the time 1 complete this story you will know what I mean. ☺

Going back to 29th May... the day-long merrymaking was finally coming to a close, when late that night, around 10pm, Rishi received a call from his friends, asking him to join them for a quick 'boys' party'. It was too late and Rishi knew that he would not be permitted to go out at this hour. As luck would have it, Kishi's mother, |ust then, asked him to park their car inside the garage. So out went Rishi — on the pretext of parking the car — and bolting the main door of the house from outside, slowly drove away to meet his friends without informing anyone at home. Ten to fifteen minutes went by. Rishi's mum, wondering, what was taking him so long, called him on his cell phone to check where he was, when a stranger answered the phone.

Aunty (Rishi's mum) was taken by surprise, "Who is speaking? This is my son Rishi's phone."

"Ma'am," the stranger responded, "a boy is lying here by the roadside. He has met with an accident."

"What rubbish!! I must have got a wrong number. My son is downstairs," saying this, Aunty disconnected the phone.

She shared with her husband what had just happened. They tried shouting aloud from their balcony, to call Rishi, which they usually did in case one of them was downstairs, but got no response.

A little flustered by now, Aunty dialled Rishi's phone once again and the same voice answered, "Ma'am, please don't disconnect and listen to me. On the screen of this phone 'home' is flashing, which means you ace this boy's family. Please listen carefully, Ma'am. We saw a boy lying unconscious, half on the road, half stuck in a car, "which has toppled over the sidewalk. We don't know who he is, but we have rushed him to the nearest hospital. I am giving you the hospital's address. Please come here quickly."

Aunty felt immobilized; tears in her eyes, she asked, "What is he wearing and what car was he in?" The answer snatched away the earth from below her feet.

"It's Rishi," she cried. "We are coming. Please stay in the hospital with him. We are just coming."

There was complete panic. They ran to the door, only to find it locked trom outside. The neighbours were called for help and one of them, who happened to be a doctor in the army, opened the door and rushed them to the hospital in his own car. As they entered the hospital, a beautiful idol of Baba awaited them. Praying in their hearts, they ran inside, only to find Rishi, lying unconscious, in a pool of blood. Three strangers — I should refer to them as Baba's angels, who had carried Rishi inside — were standing next to him. The parents were devastated, inconsolable at the traumatic sight.

"This can't be happening. Please say It Is .1 bud dn-am," Autily cried.

Rishi was taken to the ICU for dressing his wounds and other immediate tests. As they waited in anxiety, the night sernitd longer than a lifetime. They prayed all night and hoped that the morning would bring in good news. Finally, the new day dawned and, to their utter disbelief, the news was far worse than they had anticipated.

"Sorry, sir, we can't do much," reported the doctor on duty. "The boy is critical. He has a serious head injury and a lot of internal bleeding. And unfortunately, we do not have sufficient facilities in our hospital to even gauge the extent of the damage. But from his condition, 1 can only tell you that he is sinking very fast and stands a very remote chance of survival. Although 1 am not sure if he'll make It, you can still Iry shifting him to a well-equipped hospital."

'Sinking'!! 'Stands a remote chance of survival'? The family was just not prepared to handle such a huge thunderbolt. Just yesterday, not even 24 hours ago, they were celeb rating Rishi's success. And now, the doctor was saying that he was critical and would not survive the accident!

Rishi was rushed to a very renowned hospital in Delhi in an ambulance where he was taken straight Into the ICU. But even here the doctors were not certain whether they would be able to save young Rishi or not. He was sinking fast.

While Rishi was fighting for his life, back at my home, the following incident occurred. My mother had gone to visit her doctor for a regular check-up. This happened to be the same doctor who, on the previous night, had driven his neighbours, the Chibbars, to Rishi. During a casual conversation, he narrated the last night's bitter, agonizing episode of Rishi's accident to Mum, who was obviously very pained to hear about the tragedy. Whenever in pain, her first thought is always ISaba. She felt, deep inside, an urge to do something, to help this ill-fated boy. So she requested her doctor for Rishi's address and contact number and, after taking it, came homy straight away. She narrated the traumatic episode to my dad and they immediately decided to send Eaba's Udi to Rishi's house.

Dad penned down a little note for the family: "We are extremely aggrieved to hear about your son Rishank and can feel your pain. We are believers of Sai Baba of Shirdi. He is our Lord, our Saviour and His Udi (Sacred Ash) is an infallible remedy. We are sending you this Udi, with all our faith. Kindly apply it on Rishank's forehead, with complete trust in Baba and touch some of it on his lips, and Baba will not disappoint you. Your son will be fine. Our prayers are with you."

The words were strong and full of conviction but at the same time my dad was in doubt and confusion, "Should we send the Udi or not?? I hope it won't offend anyone's faith or reelings. And I also hope the boy is still alive?"

My parents were still indecisive about what to do, when the phone next to them rang. As Dad picked it up, he smiled in amazement and delight. He could hear Baba's aarti from the other end of the line. He called out to my mum, "Sharda, listen to this. It's Baba's aarti. But how? Who is calling us and playing the aarti?"

The story continues and so does Baba's time-proof, fool-proof planning. It so happened that I had gone out for some work, when 1 suddenly had an urge to visit Baba's temple. As I stepped in for Baba's Jarslian, the aarti commenced. Baba's aarti was, is and will always remain exhilarating and blissful. I really wished that I had got my parents along, as they loved the aarti. Thinking of them and missing theit presence, 1 called them, so that they could at least hear it over the phone and feel happy. Since I was in the temple and loud prayers were being sung all around, I couldn't speak, and so 1 held my mobile close to the temple's microphone. © Dear Baba pulled all the strings so beautifully that in the nick of time the phone rang, as if to reaffirm their faith that their decision of sending the Udi to Rishi was right. Their fears and apprehensions took flight and soon after partaking of the divine aarti, my parents sent our helper, with the Udi and the note to the Chibbar's house.

We had no idea what happened after that but we continued to pray for Rishi. I still recall vividly, how our family and some friends who also believed in Baba, would sit down together and chant Baba's name and pray in all earnestness for a boy and a family that we had never seen or met before. Selfless prayers are the strongest prayers, w« knew. So we prayed. Praying is beautiful. It costs absolutely nothing but gives huge returns, to the one being prayed for and also to those praying.

Three days went by. We didn't have any news of Rishi. We felt a despairing urge to call the number given by the doctor to Mum Co enquire whether the Udi had reached the right hands or not and if Rishi had survived the deadly accident. But to be honest, we could not muster up the courage to call an unknown family, especially at such a critical time.

it was 2nd June, when, in the evening, our doorbell rang. An unknown face smiled at us. "1 am Rishi's mother."

We welcomed her, taken aback by her unexpected visit. She had got our address, from the note sent by Mum and Dad.

"Thanks a lot for Sai Baba's Vibhuti that you had sent," she smiled wearily, as she sat down.

"It is totally our pleasure. But how is your son now?" Dad responded.

"His head injury was very severe," Rishi's mum continued. "Blood had started oozing out even from his ears, nose and mouth, in addition to his head. And then, all of a sudden, he could not breathe. His body was in convulsions, bouncing off the bed (almost 2-3 feet high) and falling back again and again, endlessly. Doctors administered injections but still could not control it and finally gave up hope of his survival. We thought that Rishi was breathing his last and that is when 1 recalled that in my handbag was Baba's Vibhuti, sent by you. With faith in Baba and in your words, I immediately applied it on Rishi's forehead.

At that time, Rishi's body was still bouncing 2-3 feet above the bed. And it was like a miracle; the moment the Vibhuti touched his forehead, the convulsions stopped as suddenly as they had started. Rishi lay back calm; his body that had been going up in mid-air and his breath that had been coming in spasms, all settled down, back to normal. We were so grateful to Baba and to you," she smiled again.

We all smiled back in relief, our hearts still thumping — palpitating — at the speed of light. "Then what happened? How is he now?" asked my mum.

"Well, that night, he was still in the 1CU. My husband stayed back in the hospital while 1 came home with my daughter and my sister. That night...." Aunty paused and took a deep breath. She was suddenly quiet and looked as though she would choke. I don't know why, but that moment seemed painfully long. We waited with halted breath because from her eyes it was visible that whatever she was going to narrate further about Rishi was not going to be pleasant.

After the long pause and a few sips of water, she continued. "That night Rishi's condition suddenly deteriorated. His brain, which had been seriously injured in the accident, stopped functioning. Actually, 'injured' is a wrong word," she paused. "Rishi's brain had been literally 'smashed' in the accident. We still don't how because there is no one who can even tell us, how the accident happened."

Another pause, then AunLy spoke, but this time with tears in her eyes, "The doctors informed my husband that Rishi was 'Brain Dead'. His breathing was getting slower and so was his pulse. They said, 'We are sorry but we can't revive him. It is just a matter of some time till the breathing also stops. You are requested to do the necessary paperwork to claim his body and also make arrangements for the cremation.' My husband froze. You can't imagine the plight of a father who has lost his 18-year-old son."

My family and I were shattered by the news that Aunty had just shared. How could this be true, 1 wondered in my heart. Why did Hafoa's Vibhutl save Rishi in the first place, if he had to finally go? While my sister and I exchanged painful glances, Aunty, unexpectedly, spoke up again. She was reliving those traumatic moments with us. She continued, "My husband sank into the chair close by. As he fat there helplessly, instead of calling me up, he called a close friend of ours, who is a neuro-physician in the same hospital and requested him to come over, do the paperwork and complete all formalities, so that Rishi's body could be claimed for cremation. The neuro-physician and his wife rushed to the hospital around midnight and met the concerned doctor. He informed them that though Rishi was slill breathing very lightly, he was 'Brain Dead' and could not be revived.

"Our friend asked the doctor, 'Why aren't you carrying out a surgery, as a last attempt to save the boy?' The doctors responded that it would be of no use. Rishi's condition was so critical that there was no hope. 'We are doctors, not God. We wish we could have saved him but we are at this moment as helpless as you are. And even if we do carry out a surgery, it will only increase your hospital bills by a few lakhs. Rishi has gone. We understand your pain but a surgery will not help, we are sure. His brain has stopped functioning and now It's | ust a matter of a few moments before he breathes his last.'"

Tears trickled down Aunty's cheeks as she continued. "Our friend, the neuro-physician, was adamant and after consulting my husband informed the doctors that he wanted the surgery carried out, even if the only expected gain was higher hospital bills. He told the doctors, 'You may be right that the surgery is not going to help, but for some strange reason, I feel he will pull through. 1 know it is a purely emotional decision but we want you to give it your last and best shot.' So, Rishi was again taken inside the OT and the surgery commenced." Aunty paused, closed her eyes for a moment and then started again. "Back home that night, I lay in bed crying and anxious. 1 prayed to God to save my son. I would die if something would happen to my baby, but all this while, I had no idea that back at the hospital, my Rishi had been declared 'Brain Dead' and also close to completely dead."

Aunty looked at Papa and Mama, "You sent us the Vibhuti of Sai Baba, which opened our hearts to Him. We didn't know much about Sai Baba... and didn't believe too much In Him. My father used to worship Him and so I have seen His pictures and know about Him. But that is all."

We were listening patiently and attentively, still not knowing the end of what Aunty was sharing and wondering all along if the end of her narration would be the end of Rishi or the victory of faith.

"That night," Aunty continued, "when 1 fell asleep weeping, unaware of what had happened in the hospital, I had a dream. I saw an old man clad in a white robe and a white headdress sitting before me. 1 had seen Him in pictures and immediately recognized Him to be Sai Baba of Shirdi. He was sitting beneath a tree. 1 was surprised to see Rishi lying in front of Him with his head in Baba's lap. Rishi's brain was open and its parts were lying scattered all around. Baba was slowly picking up the pieces — I mean parts of Rishi's brain — one after another, and putting them back in place, inside Rishi's head. After a lot of effort, He placed all the scattered parts back inside, put together Rishi's brain and closed it. AH this while, I sat next to Him, in the dream, crying aloud and begging Him to save my son. Finally Baba, with His hand on Rishi's 'mended, patched-up head' smiled at me affectionately and spoke, 'Why do you cry in vain? Don't you see, 1 have fixed his head back? Be patient. It will take some time hut Rishi will be absolutely fine.'

"At ttiis 1 woke up with a shudder. Totally shaken up and unable to understand the dream, I sat up crying. My sister too sat up and tried consoling me but I was too fearful and distraught to listen to anyone. I immediately called up my husband, at the hospital. He did not take my call."

Our hearts stopped in anticipation but Aunty's face suddenly lit up, "He didn't take my call, because exactly at that time the doctor stepped out of the OT and told my husband, 'Mr Chibbar, it in a miracle. In the last 30 years of my career, I have carried out countless surgeries, but today I am in disbelief. The impossible has happened, thanks to your faith. Your son is fine. The operation has been successful. Young Rishi has survived and has come back from death. You will have to be patient. It will take some time. But he will recover completely.'"

Aunty was, by now, smiling and crying, all at the same time, and so were all of us. Our faith had won; Baba's love had won over death.

"My Rishi survived," Aunty smiled through her tears. "Sai Baba gave him a new life. And I have come especially to thank all of you."

We cried, we embraced, and we bowed at Baba's feet. A new Rishi was reborn, thanks to Baba's grace. The rays of His kindness had lit up a new world for the Oiibbar family. So much had happened, all a part of Baba's master plan. Mama's faith, Papa's conviction and our prayers had blessed dear Rishi with a new life. How can I praise such a merciful, marvellous God as Baba? 1 am too petty and Baba too magnificent. All I know is that Baba's Lkii is nothing but Baba Himself. Wherever the Sacred Udi reaches, I know Baba has reached. If one touch of the Udi can stop 3-feet-high convulsions and loss of breath, if one touch of Udi can bring Haba into the lives of people who never worshipped Him, if one touch of Baba's Udi could breathe life into a 'brain dead' Rishi, what more proof is needed that the Udi is empowered and brought alive by the presence of Baba's own Soul?

This was surely the beginning of Baba's grace in their life but not the end. Rishi woke up to a new dawn, alive and breathing. It would take patience and time, as prophesied by Baba and proclaimed by doctors. But what was important was that the day of Rishi's end was transformed by Baba's grace into Ihc day of new beginnings and Rishi was reborn into a new life gifted by the kind, compassionate Baba; a Baba who gives without being asked, who shares without expecting in return... whose kindness is endless, measureless.

Rishi, Blessing II: The Bowl of Benevolence

Baba came into Rishi's life and that of his family in more ways than one can imagine. It appeared as though Baba had taken full and final responsibility of the family on His own shoulders. Their troubles were no more their own but Baba's.

The biggest problem had been taken care of by Baba, but there were many more hurdles still to be faced. The next day dawned, as indicated by the doctors, to huge medical bills. The family was informed that ?15 lakh had to be deposited before noon the next day, otherwise Rishi's treatment would have to be stopped. This came as another jolt and once again stirred the ripple of panic. No middle-class family has such huge savings and that too in banks. The Chibbars were in a plight. While Rishi's dad ran to banks to gather whatever little they had as savings, his mum prayed. The day ended with a negligible collection.

Aunty's tears were back again as she slept to another helpless night. But on this night she said a small prayer of request to the new God in her life, "Baba, please help us. You have blessed Rishi with a new life. Now You can't let his treatment stop. Only You can show the way out of this huge problem. We must have?! 5 lakh in our bank by noon tomorrow. Please, Baba,"

And she slept... only to meet Baba in her dreams once again; lucky lady, in the midst of unlucky situations. © On this night, He walked in her dream, with a deep, big vessel full of coins. As He walked, coins fell out of the vessel, which was loaded to the brim.

"Baba," cried Amita Aunty. "Baba, I need money for my son's treatment. Please help me."

Baba stopped, turned back and smiled, "Why do you cry, when I am there? Keep collecting all that falls out of my vessel *id your problem shall be solved."

So, Aunty treaded behind Baba, collecting all that fell, in her dupatta. She woke up the next morning, very positive and energized, reached the hospital and spoke to Uncle, "Baba's coming in my dream, for the first time, was very auspicious. Our Rishi came back from death. And I saw Him again last night, that too with money overflowing. 1 am sure it is a good sign."

Uncle agreed, "You are right, Amita. Your seeing the dream is surely auspicious but we still don't have one-tenth of the amount needed. What should I do?"

They sat and discussed the problem and then Aunty suddenly had a good idea, "Why don't you speak to their accounts department and request them for some additional time? If we have time on hand and Rishi's treatment continues, we will find a way nut."

Uncle liked the idea and immediately left to meet the concerned person.

It was haif past 12. He went up to the lady at the Help Desk. "My son is in the ICU and has undergone a surgery and we have been asked to deposit ?15 lakh at the payment counter by noon today, But I need a few minutes to discuss something with you, please."

"Sure, sir," she smiled. "Before that, can 1 have the patient's name?"

"Yes, yes, sure. He is Rishi Chibbar," responded Uncle anxiously.

She was still looking into her computer when she spoke, "Yes, sir. Thanks a lot. We have received the payment of ?15,50,000. Now you have a surplus balance of ?SO,000. How else can 1 help you?"

"WHAT??" exclaimed Uncle. "Surplus?? Please check again. That must be a mistake."

She checked and checked. But there was no mistake. Another miracle had happened in less than 24 hours. ☺ The money had been deposited in their account, before noon, that too in excess of what was needed and they had no clue how. They came to know later that several family friends, old employers and cousins had deposited huge amounts to help them in this traumatic phase, without as much as informing them. Baba's light had touched each of their hearts and inspired such a nobfe, selfless and most unexpected act. The money was there, as reassured by Baba in the dream. ☺

His ways, only He knows. To someone addicted to drinking, He would appear in his dream, sit on his chest and press it hard, till the person promised to give up drinking. To those with wicked, impious thoughts, He would argue with them and ask them questions in their dream, till they realized their mistake and promised to give up their vices. So also, our Rishi was healed and brought back from the dark tunnel of death by none other than Baba Himself. It must have been the good karnias of the family that Baba reached them right on time to ward off ail their misfortunes. Rishi is truly only Baba's child now. His life, his existence, his breath... all belong to Baba. ☺

Rishi, Blessing III: Rishi's Path Crosses Mine and Changes the Course of my Life

Rishi is probably the next big reason after Babaji and my parents that made me intensely spiritual, that taught me to connect deeper, that brought out the healer in me and that gave a new, beautiful direction to my life. Meeting Rishi marked the beginning of not just a new chapter in my life, hut it was almost like being reborn to a new spiritual me.

I met Rishi for the first time in my life, when he was brought home, after his accident. As I walked into the room, excited at meeting Baba's Miracle Child... 1 was stunned. On the bed lay a heaped agglomeration of bones.... Yes, that was Rishi. I could see no skin, only a heap of bones. His head was tilted to a side as he had lost control on even that and saliva drooled out of his mouth. 1 stood still. I had expected to see a young boy back from hospital, not a pack of bones. But unfortunately, that was his condition.

His eyes looked at me questioningly. I walked close to him and spoke, "I am Diili, Rishi, Puja Didi (I am addressed as Puja at home). Sai Baba has sent me to you. You will be fine. I promise, Please have faith."

The eyes smiled back. That is when I realized that Rishi had, along with many other things, lost the power to speak as well. A few months went by, Kishi was now out of danger but was totally bedridden. The right side of his body was paralysed; he could not move and he could

not speak... my heart ached each time ! saw him.
One day, he desperately tried to convey something to his mum but since he couldn't speak or use sign language, he was miserable. She gave him at least ten options so as to figure out what he wanted to say, but it was no use. Finally out of frustration, Rishi started banging his head, which was the only part of his body that he could by now control, against the wall.

Aunty called me in panic, "Puja, he is banging his head against the wall, and not stopping. He is crying. I don't know what to do."

"Give him some Udi mixed in water, quickly," I replied.

And the moment the Udi mixture went down his throat, Rishi calmed down. He lay back, looking at the rubelight in the room. And that is when his mum realized that all he wanted was that the lights of his room be switched off. How helpless life makes us....

It was 5th October. I had requested a few friends to organize a Bha/an Sandhya in Rishi's house. I have always believed that generating positive energy through honest, selfless prayers is magical. And the magic becomes even bigger when the chief magician is Baba Sai. A beautiful durbar of Baba's innumerable pictures was set up in the living room of Rishi's house. Baba's face shone in all its resplendence and glory, behind the many lamps and diyas. The echo of the devotional songs reverberated through the house... right to the room where Rishi lay in bed. As 1 sat before this celestial mix of light, sound and glory, I felt Baba's picture turning real... alive.

And Baba spoke to me, "Heal Rishi, Puja."

Tears clouded my eyes, "What can I do, Baba? He's in such a bad condition."

Baba smiled, "Go and pray, and heal him."

I broke down before Baba. "Baba, please don't give me such a tough task. I am apprehensive that I may be ridiculed, if I can't do much."

His eyes smiled, "Don't you have faith in Me?"

I wept on, "1 do, Baba, I have complete faith. It is jidt that I have never undertaken a task so big and mystic."

He flashed His 'smile-to-die-for' once again, © "There has to be a first time, my child. Go, have faith. I shall heal." His words were piercing, reassuring and compelling; my mind was made up. I had to do this.

After a few days I requested Rishi's parents, "If you don't mind, I'd like to come and do some 'healing' on Rishi. 1 have a 'gift to heal' from Baba, and He wants me to use my gift to help Rishi."

They were delighted, "Of course, please do. We'll be grateful."

So, 1 walked into Rishi's room on 1st November, to begin my healing... but where do I start?? Every little part of his body was badly affected by the accident. I stood there, praying to Baba, "Where should 1 begin, Baba?" At the same time, 1 prayed for inner strength. Weak-hearted me was too shaky to even touch Rishi, in his present condition.

I walked up closer, as Rishi looked at me with the same questioning eyes. He wanted to say something but I didn't know what. He looked at me helplessly and I looked at him, even more helpless. But someone was watching over both of us and He was certainly not helpless. © He had His plans ready, 1 am sure.

1 affectionately put my aim around Rishi's neck to support him, as he lay in bed. My other hand, as if lifted by Baba, slowly landed on Rishi's throat. "You must speak, Rishi. You just have to. You can't spend the rest of your life without a voice. You have to help me, so that we um do this together. 1 will pray to heal your throat and bring back your voice, but you will have to work really hard to speak and also pray along with me."

As I stopped speaking, Rishi gave me his sweetest smile, which said It all. He was ready and so was I. ☺

While Rishi and 1 were busy making plans of getting his lost voice back, the doctors had other plans. Rishi's parents were handed a document by his doctors, a document that stated the impossible: a document that informed them that their son would now, in this life, never be able to speak again. In layman's language, it stated that during the critical brain surgery, Rishi's 'voice-box' had to be removed, as it was badly damaged. And without a voice box, we apparently don't have a voice... which goes to say that Rishi was medically termed to live voiceless for the rest of his life. But thankfully. Rishi and I knew nothing of this. So, while the doctors did their work, Rishi and I did ours. I prayed resolutely, Rishi struggled determinedly and Baba graced assiduously. By the end of my healing session that day, I felt Rishi was whispering but I could see from the faces of the family, they thought I was imagining. I left after praying.

1 went back on 7th November, after a week. Rishi flashed a huge, happy smile on seeing me. That day as 1 put my hands on Rishi's throat — which had a hole drilled into it, for some medical reasons — 1 felt intense warmth in my palms. To be honest, 1 felt Baba's presence in the room. I saw showers of light and 1 realized that His hand was on my hand. © I prayed, Rishi struggled far more than before. "Rishi, say 'Daba'... please, you can do this." He twisted and turned in bed as though wriggling to throw his locked voice out.

And then, I heard a whisper... a soft whisper, though no voice still. "Baba," he whispered with all his might.

It was such an encouraging moment. Rishi's parents looked on. Their faith was so firm that they told me nothing about the medical reports. And thank God for that, as it may have lessened the intensity of my faith.

It was 13th November, evening. I had just come back from Rishi's house. His whispers were louder today but they were still whispers. I could not bear to see Rishi writhing in an urge to speak up, looking at me with such faith and still not being able to speak. It was killing me. I reached home and went straight to the temple room in our house. There 1 sat down before Baba's idol and began chanting Baba's Gayatri Mantra, with a madness of sorts. The rosary (jaapnutald) was in my hand and I decided to do the stipulated 108 jaaps (chants). It took me very long. But burning with the deep desire to hear Rishi speak, I chanted aloud in an all-consuming reverence:

"Aunt Shri Shirdi Vaasaaye Vidmahe, Sachidanandaaye Dili Mahi, Tanno Sai Prachodayath."

The more I chanted, the more fierce and passionate my prayers grew and the more healing energy J sent out to Rishi. After a 'full-of-faith' prayer evening, I slept, only to be blessed by Baba. Yes, I heard His voice, though I am not sure, to this day, whether the voice was in my dream state or in my semi-conscious state. But I heard Him say, "Rishi will speak."

Next day, 14th November, early morning, 1 called Rishi's mum brimming with faith, "Aunty, Rishi will speak. Baba has assured."

A few hours later, around 11am, my phone rang. It was Rishi's mum. I received the call, only to hear her weeping aloud. She was sobbing into the phone.

1 got scared, "What's happened? Please, tell me. Aunty, stop crying, please. Is Rishi okay?"

She sobbed louder, "Here... speak," she said, between her sobs.

Before 1 could understand what she meant, a voice echoed into my phone, "Puja Didi."

OH BABA SAI!! That was Kishi. Soon I wab crying, my mum, my

sis... we were all crying, while Papa was smiling gratefully. I drove like a maniac to Rishi's house, along with my family. We cried, we laughed; we celebrated Baba's love, Baba's grace...

I came to know a few days later about that medical report when Rishi's dad informed me that some doctors wanted to speak to me, to find out how I did the impossible. 1 became famed as a healer. People thought I was gifted with miraculous healing abilities. But no one knew the truth. 1 did nothing. My Baba healed, my Baba blessed, my Baba graced... Who am I to heal anyone? But His love brings out the innate godly ability to heal, in inept people like me. How can I thank Baba enough? That day a new 'me' was born... exploding with faith, as never before. My meditation on Baba grew apace and the purpose of my life slowly unfolded before me. I was sure that the rest of my life would be spent loving and serving Baba, healing pain and suffering and adding smiles to as many hearts as possible. And that is what I do today and i iove this life, which is a gift of Baba. ©

Rishi is much better now. He walks, he talks, he sings, he smiles and he lives by his Baba's name. Innocently, unknowingly, young Rishi gave a new direction to my life. And I must share with all of you that though Rishi's right hand is still paralysed, he has helped me type-in this book. All loose sheets of papers, scattered thoughts, innumerable diaries, have been patiently keyed into the computer — using the left hand — by none other than Baba's boy, Rishi. Thank you, Rishi, for helping me make this book happen.... May Baba's grace and the blessings of the readers heal you and your paralysis, completely.

1 bow before You, my Baba Sai. There is no worry, no concern now. The lesson is clear; the questions have been answered. The path to salvation goes through Shirdi. No rituals, no religious practises, no outward formalities are needed. Only complete faith and surrender in our Guru, Baba's feet shall bestow upon us Light and lead us on the Golden Path... into His arms, unto His feet. Aum Sai Ram...

Aum Sai Shri $ai faya Jaya Sai

"This is our Dwarkamai, where you are sitting. She wards offa.ll dangers and anxieties of the children who sit in her lap. This Masjidmai is very merciful; she is the merciful mother of the simple devotees, whom she will save in calamities. Once a person sits in her lap, his troubles are over. He who rests in gets Bliss."

— SAI BABA OF SHIRDI

In the Hands of Sai

"I require no door to enter. I haw no form; 1 always live everywhere. As a wirepuller, I carry on all the actions of the man who trusts Me and merges in Me."

He, who could keep lamps burning with water and without oil, He, who could know the past, present and future of a person without even meeting him, He, who could take the form of any God, any Saint, any Guru, merely at will... had to be the Lord God Himself. This kind God blessed the sacred land of Shirdi and anyone who turned to Him for help.

When the world slept, He was wide awake, looking to the problems and troubles of His children, far and wide. His devotees, out of great love, got for Him, a wooden plank to sleep upon. Baba tied this plank to the rafters of the ceiling, with torn, worn-out rags. It was a marvel that the rags could sustain the weight of the plank; wonder of wonders, how they sustained Baba's weight as well. Baba kept lamps burning all night long, on the four corners of this plank and was forever wide awake. God does not need sleep or rest. God does not know taste or distaste. God is beyond night or day. He was present everywhere, lovingly ate whatever was offered and reached His children whenever and whatever time- they called out to Him.

When I set about collecting Baba's miracles, stories, experiences and teachings at Shirdi, my first story came from a warm, elderly, sophislicaLed gentleman called Chandrasekhar, who must be older than my own father. He shared with me his extraordinary experience, something! had never heard or read before. He had lived through very deep spiritual experiences impelled by Baba, had been profoundly transformed by them and veered briskly towards spirituality. Not only had Baba taken him on an inward journey but had also blessed him with a new life. In fact, if it were not for dear Baba, Chandrasekhar

Uncle may not have been sitting next to me that day arift sharing his experiences.

By the grace of Baba, Chandrasekhar Uncle had bought a new house on coming back from a long job assignment afcr Kuwait. He was overwhelmed at finally possessing a house that he could call his own. He .smilingly told me that he looked after his house like his baby, taking special care to keep it spotless and sparkling. One rainy day, as Uncle was taking a stroll in his garden, he observed huge leaves from a coconut tree, overlapped on an electric wire, right in front of the house. The wire was high up, connecting two eiectric poles. Keen to bring back orderliness in his garden, Uncle thought of calling someone to help push the leaves off the cable. But unable to find any help around, he decided to do this himself. He brought a rather tall ladder, fixed it up against the pole and slowly climbed up, chanting Baba's name.

When Uncle was narrating this incident to me, his eyes grew big and sparkled mischievously and he said, "I wasn't alone. I knew Sai was with me."

So, dear Uncle climbed right up the ladder and tried to push the coconut leaves down with the help of a stick. ! must share with the readers that when Chandrasekhar Uncle was trying these precarious aerobatics, he was 70+ years of age! ☺

He was at a great height now and was exerting all possible force to shove off the huge leaves from the wire.

"Help me, Baba," he was insisting.

He attempted yet again, with all his might. In doing so, he pushed his body backward to draw more force, lost his balance and before he knew, he was falling backwards from the ladder towards the ground.

"This is my end," was his first thought. He articulated his flurry of emotions to me, while sharing this terrifying incident. "In those few moments of my fall, several thoughts passed in a flash across my mind. Will I survive this accident? And even if 1 do, would my old bones ever he able to cope with the injuries? What will happen to my wife?? Who will look after her in this old age??" As these thoughts clouded his mind with fear, he evoked his Sai for help. "Baba!" he called aloud.

And lo! Just one call of faith and what was this that he suddenly felt on his back? He could clearly sense two strong hands under him. The hands quickly and suddenly straightened him from his horizontal falling posture to a vertical position and within moments, his feet touched the ground. And what was this?? He was standing straight; unhurt and free from even the slightest scratch, forget the broken bones! As he regained his breath, he unconsciously and gratefully uttered "Sainath" and immediately turned around to see who had been sent by his Sai to save him. His searching eyes looked around with tearful gratitude... but who should he have thanked?? Voila!! What was this... magic, miracle or dream?? Who should Uncle have thanked?? For he was all alone in his beautiful garden.

Uncle was initially in a state of grave shock, which slowly transformed into a happy surprise; for there was no one around whom he could possibly thank. 1 le was all alone and there was not the faintest sign of anyone's presence. Those powerful hands that had taken all his weight and slowly lowered him onto the ground were the hands of his Baba Sai. ☺

1 smiled in amazement as a thought passed through my mind. 1 have written in several poetic invocations dedicated to my Big Daddy, my Tather Sai, that **when we are treading the most treacherous and trying, thorn-laden paths of our lives, Baba does not merely walk along as our biggest strength and support, but rather lifts us up in His warm, loving arms, till we cross over from the deadly thorns to the bed of roses.** And here I was, witness to an actual, literal translation of my words into reality. Baba had taken Uncle in His all-powerful arms and saved his life. My inner core

trembles at the depth of Baba's love for His children. He does just about anything for those who trust Him wholeheartedly.

Uncle told me with a tearful smile, during our conversation at Shirdi that lie could feel those hands very intensely, even n#w, each time he recalled the incident. Baba not only blessed him with a new life but also reaffirmed his faith... **"Call me once, only once with love and I'll cross a million oceans to save you." © Miracles are created every moment, every day in our lives, so long as we breathe our prayers with love and faith.**

This is not all. Chandrasekhar Uncle's wife was also an ardent devotee of Baba. When I met him at Shirdi, sometime in the beginning of 2006, he told me that he had read the Sai Satcharita 2S5 times in the last four years. He smiled very sweetly when he told me that he had the habit of counting and making a note each time he read the Satcharita. I guess, we all have our unique ways of loving Baba and this was Uncle's special way. © What left me even more amazed was that Aunty (his wife) had read the Satcharita far more number of times than he had... though, of course, she had not counted her readings. Such was Baba's importance in their life. Each breath they took was a dedication in their Baba's feet.

The Sai Satcharita is Baba's second gift to humankind, the first being the Sacred Udi. My personal experience stands proof that **the Satcharita is like a magic potion or a wish-fulfilling wand... ask and it shall be granted... pray and it shall he yours. Just hold the Satcharita close to your heart, make a wish and then read it with faith... and then what is impossible to the world shall become possible for you.**

I have realized and learnt over these years of knowing Baba that there is nothing more powerful than reading about Baba's life and His teachings. It truly has a life-transforming impact. **Reading about Baba is equivalent to being in His Divine Presence. It is like spending hours in meditative oneness with Him. It is the**

easiest path to follow in this difficult life and this complicated world. Just read about Baba, with faith and with love and all that you pray for shall be yours. This is the pure thought that inspired my book. I thought, if I could bring into the hands of Baba's children another sacred text similar to the Satcharita, it would bring so much more joy and bliss in their lives. So here is another opportunity, direct in your hands, to get 'all' you wish for, by just reading about Baba and staying connected with Him. So read and read, absorb every good thought, every positive teaching, get rid of every pain and welcome happiness into your life.

Baba's love is so beautiful... it comes back manifold to His devotees. He always gives indications and signs in His special way to show acceptance of our love and confirmation of our faith and that is exactly what He did with Chandrasekhar Uncle and Aunty. They kept reading the Satcharita and Baba kept blessing them in return. Soon, their house was vibrating with positive energy. **Any place where love, faith and prayers for Baba dwell, becomes His Dwarkamai.** And that is exactly what happened to their house. Baba started appearing on a wall in their house, sitting in His cross-legged posture, on the Dwarkamai stone. It was pure magic. No pen or pencil was used, nor did anyone sketch anything. But if anyone would look with faith at the plain white wall in Chandrasekhar Uncle's house, Baba would become clearly visible and would smile back. Uncle told me that his house was frequented by many people, who wanted to seek Baba's blessings and witness this remarkable spectacle.

Faith and love for Baba comes back to the devotees as boundless blessings in one form or another. His appearing on a wall in their house was Baba's way of strengthening their faith in His Holy Feet. **The Satcharita is strength, it is power. It can fulfil each and every desire, if read with love. It is priceless and invaluable. Sincere reading, supplemented by true devotion can even bring us back from the stronghold of death. So ask of Baba what you wish for and read the Satcharita daily with faith. A Saptah — completing the Satcharita reading within a week — bestows**

upon the reader health, wealth, peace, joy and success. And a Chalisa — completing the Satcharita reading within forty days and lighting a lamp before Baba each day — bequeaths bliss in life and salvation in after-life, for the reader. Such is the power in reading Baba's life, teachings and blessings. We have in our hands a treasure grove of bliss and enlightenment, gifted by none other than Baba Sai Himself.

Aum Sal Shri Sai faya faya Sai

"Unless there is some relationship or connection, nobody goes anywhere. If tiny men or creatures come to you, do not discourteously drive them away, but receive them well find treat them with due respect. Shri Hari (God) will be certainly pleased, if you give water to the thirsty, bread to the hungry, clothes to the naked, and your verandah to strangers for resting. If anybody wants any money from you, and you are not inclined to give, do not give, but do not bark at him, like a dog. Let anybody speak hundreds of things against you, do not resent by giving any bitter reply. If you always tolerate such things, you will certainly be happy."

— SAI BABA OF SHIRDI

Come, Sit and Chit-chat with Me, Baba

It is said in the Shruti (Veda) that Puja of the Gods is not complete, unless a golden coin was offered. The Shastras have laid it down that, when one goes to see God, King, Saint or Guru, one should not go empty-handed. One should offer something, preferably money. The Taittiriya Upanishad says, "Give with faith, give with magnanimity, give with modesty, with awe and with sympathy."

Sai Baba was an embodiment of the Vedas. His mere contact could impart lessons that all the Vedas, Upanishads and other Holy Scriptures put together could not. His words rained nectar and His teachings were — and still are — the pathways to happiness. He takes away the sufferings and troubles of all those devotees who believe in Him completely and abide by His instructions. Baba's teachings are innumerable but one lesson that He considered to be of prime importance was regarding Values and Valuables. Values imply virtues and inner goodness in a human being, whereas Valuables imply material wealth and money.

In the present Kali Yuga, everyone gives utmost importance to money. The reason is thai today we cannot survive without it. from basic necessities to topmost luxuries, it is all a piay of money and that is why most of us have come to believe that the sole aim of our lives is the accumulation of wealth. At the same time, many wise and learned men feel that money is the evil behind all problems and is also the main cause behind suffering. Vices like greed, dishonesty, hatred, hostility and even murder are by-products of 'our unappeasable appetite for money'. This endless want creates disputes even within close-knit families and results in such deep-rooted animosity that those born of the same blood are ready to take lives for it. So bitterly ingrained are the evils associated with wealth.

Yet, the fact remains that money by Itself is not evil. It is the right use 01 misuse of money, which makes it favourable or malicious. **Baba has said in the Sai Satcharita, "Wealth should be the means to work out Dharma. If it is used for personal enjoyment it is wasted."**

The same truth has been highlighted beautifully in Hindu scriptures. Goddess Lakshmi is the personification of Wealth and Lord Narayan is the embodiment of Virtues. Lord Narayan is more popularly referred to as Lakshmi Narayan. The reason for this is that Goddess Lakshmi and Lord Narayan are said to be two bodies but one soul and are regarded as inseparable. Baba's advice mentioned above is echoed by the following example of Lakshmi Narayan.

In the kali Yuga, every individual is in a race to acquire wealth and riches. In scriptural terms, this implies that everyone is praying to Goddess Lakshmi and requesting her in all earnestness to come and live in his/her home. And when the prayers are sincere, Goddess Lakshmi does come to live in the devotee's home. But since Lakshmi and Narayan are inseparable, when we seek Lakshmi alone, She does answer our prayers and resides with us in the form of wealth, affluence and prosperity but She doesn't stay for too long. She is lonely without Her consort, Lord Narayan, and soon goes back to Him. So, when She suddenly leaves the devotee's home, very obviously all that is left behind is sorrow, suffering and scarcity.

But when a devotee seeks not just Lakshmi alone, but seeks both Lakshmi and Narayan together, the result is complete bliss. The reason is that when Lakshmi enters a devotee's home accompanied by Narayan, they stay on forever, blessing the devotee with love, happiness and prosperity. This implies that **when wealth is only used for personal enjoyment and luxurious living, it does not stay for long and gets wiped out over a period of time. When the**

same wealth (Lakshmi accompanied by Narayan, Who signifies virtuous use of wealth) is also used for good causes, virtuous deeds and righteous activities, it always stays with the devotee and also becomes the means for inner and outer gains, both spiritual as well as material. So always remember Sai's teachings and use the wealth you possess to work out Dharma. Worldly Valuables must always be accompanied by soulful Values and then only do they become supremely powerful and last to eternity. This one teaching of Baba, if followed sincerely, will cleanse away all sorrows and sufferings and make our present and our future both blissful and beautiful.

Now let us take a journey to heaven....

The dawn of a beautiful morning, dewdrops on petals, the fragrance of incense sticks, bliss, peace, serenity, love and holy chants — the place has to be Shirdi... so enthralling and enchanting are the wee hours of Shirdi that words fail to describe the ecstasy of those divine moments. Visualize the Kakail Aarti (Morning Prayer): thousands of devotees singing together in unison and requesting liaba to wake up to their calls of love, several pandits bathing His life-size sparkling-white idol, dressing Him up, adorning Him and making Him look like the King who rules the entire universe — it is all so beautiful, so joyful that one feels as though he is in seventh heaven. To a devotee, nowhere in this world can there be a morning more beautiful than each and every morning of Shirdi. Imagine the soft breeze blowing past your face and smelling of Sai; imagine the peaceful silence of the morning and even this silence reverberates the name ot Sai: you close your eyes and still there is light; you are all alone hut still there is the sensation of a million forms of Sai around you, within you. Can there be a daybreak more beautiful, can there he a heart more peaceful, can there be a love more captivating? No, there can't he, because there is only one Sai and only one Shirdi and this is our Sai's Shirdi, our Shirdi.

The Kakad Aarti had just finished. I bowed before Baba's celestial form in the Samadhi Mandir at Shirdi and with tears flowing ceaselessly from my eyes, stepped out into the daylight. It was impossible to control the outburst of tears because that one hour spent in the Samadhi Mandir with Baba churns up emotions, and turns it all upside down. There is something in the air, which makes you irrepressibly emotional and sensitive. And then there is Baba's life-size idol, smiling at you with the most captivating smile, as if in the very next minute He is going to step down from His throne and walk towards you. God!! My heart skips a beat even as I pen down those sacred feelings. So that one hour is the best time to wash your eyes of all toxins and cleanse your heart out. I was in the same state when 1 stepped out of the temple. Drenched in showers of the rain called Baba, I walked towards the high platform next to the Samadhi Mandir and sat down, all alone. My tears had still not stopped their journey to the outside world. How could they; they were tears of Jove and when love for your God, your Sai, is overflowing through your very being, the tears have no option but to pour out.

I closed my eyes; I could feel my Baba, my Father in every iota of my existence. I was overwhelmed with emotions and all I wished for was to merge in Him. I didn't want to spend even a single moment away from Him or His divine form in the Samadhi Mandir. My mind was restless and my heart ached for His presence close to me. My entire being was pulsating with Baba's love.

Still with my eyes shut, I spoke to Him with childlike persistence, "Baba 1 love you and I can't live without You even for a single moment. There are thousands of people queued up for Your darshan, so 1 can't even come back inside the Samadhi Mandir. This is not fair. I have come to meet You from far away and I can't even spend quality time with You. This is just not fair. I am Your daughter, Your child. The least I deserve is Your company, Baba. So now it is Your turn. I am very lonely and very sad. 1 can't come inside the Mandir to meet You hut I'm sure You can come outside to meet me. So please, Baba, come to me. I'm waiting. Please Baba, please don't break my heart. I'll keep sitting here all day, but will not get up without meeting You. Come, sit and chit-chat with me for some time, Baba. I'm waiting and I love You a lot, Baba. Love You! Please mine, sit anil chit-chat with me for sonic time, Baba." I may be sounding like a maniac but Baba's love is so overpowering (as all His devotees will agree) that I was just not in my senses.

I was totally lost in Him, merged in a deep meditative oneness and still repeating my request on and on, like a little child yearning for chocolates, "Baha, please come, sit and chit-chat with «ie for some time. Please, Baba," when 1 distinctly heard an elderly voice, "Maa!!" 1 opened my eyes with a shudder. Next to me was an old man, clad as a sadliu, "Maa," he repeated, "Do you mind If 1 sit down and chit-chat with you for some time?"

1 died; I truly did!! I froze at the spot!! 1 could not believe this was actually happening and was completely disoriented and lost. I was calling Baba but I was really not expecting someone, who resembled Him so closely, in age and attire to walk up to me and repeat my subconscious words back to me consciously. Godl! No, I really wasn't!!

What was 1 supposed to understand? Was this Baba? Had He actually come to meet me? Why had he, this sadhu, repeated the very words — Do you mind if 1 sit down and chit-chat with you for some time — that I had spoken in my heart? How did he know what I was thinking? Was this merely a coincidence? Or was this Baba... my Baba and I could not even recognize Him?

He looked at my blank, expressionless face and repeated yet again, "Maa, may 1 sit down and chat with you for a while?"

in the midst of my turbulent emotions, I finally responded, "Yes, Baba, please sit down."

He sat down on the steps next to me and started talking. "1 have come from very far," he said. "My arm got injured on the way."

Saying this, he pulled out his hand and arm, which were bruised and looked somewhat burnt all over. Then he continued to describe to me how the injury took place and certain other things as well, but I can't recall a single word today. 1 was too dazed to absorb what he spoke.

There was a battle going on In my head: Is he Baba or is my imagination running too wild? Had Baha actually heard my prayers?? Was all this merely 3 dream or for real?'/ I needed someone to pinch me.

But in all the chaos of my Intertwining thoughts, I do recall one thing that he finally said: "Maa, can you please give me f 100 so that I can get my arm treated and also have something us eat?"

Can you imagine... my suspicious, miser brain told mv that 1 would Ju- an absolute fool to believe him. Why should 1 pay him? Would Balm ask me for money??

Well, very truly has Baba said, "Where there is faith, there can't be doubt. And where there is doubt, there can't be faith." 1 was inoM certainly in doubt and the faith and love with which I had called oui to Baba were totally amiss. Greed and selfishness had overpowered love. While 1 was contemplating what to do, I noticed my cousin Sunll, who had gone to the hotel, walking towards me. He first looked at me with raised eyebrows and then at the old man with questioning eyes.

All I said was, "The Baba wants some money."

Before 1 could speak further, my cousin opened his fist and in his palm was a ?5-coin, which he quickly handed over to the old man and said, "Go, Baba, and have a cup of tea."

The old man smiled at him, stood up and turned towards me, "Ok, Maa, I'll leave now. 1 had a nice chat with you. Thanks! Be happy till eternity."

Saying this, he slowly walked off.

As 1 looked at him walk away, sudden realization dawned upon me. Oh God! Why was he calling me Maa? In the Sai Satctiarita it is mentioned that Baba used to address all women as Maa. And this elderly sadhu had been addressing me as Maa throughout the conversation. Was that a hint to me that I didn't catch? My gaze was still following the old man when I again observed: a jtioli (cloth bag) on his shoulder, a future! (tin-pot) in his hand and a satka (short stick) under his arm. He wore a kaftti (a-long, flowing coat-like dress) and had around his head a bandana-like cloth. Oh God! That was Baba! It had to be Him!! The jholi, the tumrel and the satka were the three things that Baba always carried with Him. And, of course, he was dressed exactly like Baba and he even kept addressing me as Maa. Then the final realization shook me. Baba had pushed His arm through burning hot flames to save a child when He was living in Shirdi. Those burns never did heal completely and continued to be treated by His devotee, till He passed away. And this old Baba had shown me the same burns and injuries on his arm. Oh God!! That was Baba!

Thoughts flashed through rny head like electric currents, Why were all the realizations happening now, when He was walking away? 1 am the one who so affectionately called out to Him and when He came 1 didn't recognize Him. My God, what a blunder I had committed! I felt tears pricking my eyes. I madly dug my hand into my wallet, pulled out a noo-note and ran after the Baba to give Him the tiaksliina that He had asked for lovingly. But alas!! He was nowhere to be seen. In those few seconds, He had embraced the nothingness nf the breeze. I searched and searched but in vain. There was no saiihu, no old man, no Baba anywhere. Baba had gone as easily and quickly as He had come. And 1 had failed, miserably failed, not only in recognizing Him but my faith too had failed. I was ashamed, abashed.

I can never forgive myself to this day. Never! And that is why 1 am sharing my experience with all of you. I'lease don't ever make the mistake of not recognizing your Baba. **Baba most certainly comes running to His children when they call out to Him with pure, undiluted love. He needs no conveyance, nor any open doors to walk in. All He needs is a heart overflowing with love and a**

devotee replete with faith. He comes in any form, any [materialization. We must identify Him by using our heart and surely Jnot our head. 1 used my head and 1 went wrong. So wrong!! How I wish even today that I had heard the voice of my heart, which kept ..repeating, "This has to he Baba!"

A petty amount of ?100 had won the battle within my junk-filled head. I still can't come to terms with the fact that 1 refused the elderly, Injured Baba a measly amount of money. Lucky Sunil had made an offering unknowingly and it was accepted with love. The old man took il with grace and didn't even ask for more. And I was asked for it and I refused! That, too, when 1 clearly knew that Baba, even when in flesh and blood, asked for dakshina from His devotees to teach them the lesson of detachment. He accepted donations and charities but kept no money In Ills own possession for more than a few moments. The annum I .muinulated was immediately distributed either as meals or as blus'.liiK'. 1o Ills needy children. At the same time, Baba promised that lIn- Rlwr would In* benefitted multifariously. **He always said, "The giver sows a wed, only to reap a rich harvest in the future. Give one receive manifold,"**

On certain occasions. Baba even asked for dakshina from those who had made promises or taken oaths and forgotten about them — and thereby delivered them freedom from old bondages or burdens. And here was silly me.... who would normally not think twice before feeding the poor or helping the needy. I could anyway have given the amount to Hie old Baha so that He could have treated His arm. But I failed miserably and I want to make sure that no one else does!! **I am not prescribing that money be distributed freely or blindly if anyone asks for it.... All I am saying in that the discretion of the heart be used at subliminal moments.**

However, I did learn a happy lesson on love from my Baba. I learnt that if He was kind enough to appear just to make me smile, He would surely reach me, when I was In pain. **One call and He would answer... One paryer and He would fulfil.** I was soaked soul-deep in His love and He actually manifested as the elderly Baba to keep my faith. So merge in Him with purity and nothing would then be unattainable, Trust Him beyond question, beyond all doubt because,- He Himself has said, **"I man I test myself, where there is complete faith."** So love Him, trust Hint and stay prepared at every moment, for you never know when He may walk up to you and say, "Oh Maa, Oh Bapu, may I sit with you and chit-chat for some time?" ©

Aum Sai Shri Sai Jaya Jaya Sai

"Why should you take the responsibility of the actions on you'? Do not entertain the sense of doer-ship in doing good, as well as for bad deeds; be entirely prideless and egoless in all things and thus your spiritual progress will be rapid."

— SAI BABA OF SHIRDI

The Shri Sai Satcharita: A Jewel in the Crown of Baba

"Why do you prostrate yourself now and then? One Nantaskar offered with love and humility is enough."

Baba's love is so wonderful. He not only initiates us on the path of spirituality and inner growth but also takes care of all our worldly dealings and worries. When in Shirdi, Baba had saved a devotee, Damu Anna, from major losses in business. A broker had suggested to Damu Anna that he should invest in cotton speculation, as this would earn him huge profits. But Baba did not allow this. Damu Anna was initially disillusioned as In though! Dut his hopes of earning huge profits were dashed to the ground. Hut later, he didn't have enough words to thank Baba when he came to know that the broker had carried out the same speculation business with another merchant who had suffered huge losses; such is the grandeur of Baba; His unconditional love has no parallel, no comparison. **He runs to His children, whatever the reason... be it diseases, emotional traumas, financial conderns or a quest for higher knowledge. He is always there to heal, provide, protect or guide.**

Baba's satcharita is like a resh-water spring that not only allays our thirst but also adds sweetness to the satiation. If we read the Satcharita with Sharaddha, continue that reading with Saburi and keep our trust in Baba;s Udi... no goal is too far, no dream too big. We give up our faith too easily and give up our patience too quickly. But if we are persistent and full of faith, nothing can stop us from touching the stars and turning our dreams into reality.

Baba has taught me that running away from pain or problems can never be a solution because they will follow us wherever we try to escape. The solution is 'facing the problem with faith and fortitude and looking at it right in the eye'. We can scare our problems away if we have faith, inner strength and forbearance. The more we fear them, the more they chase us. The stronger our faith, the quicker and easier it is to chase them away. Here is a living proof of faith, patience and inexplicable love; and also a sparkling evidence of the power of the Satcharittt; the more the reading, the greater the blessing.

This story, of a devotee's willpower and Baba's gracious love revolves around my friend Amillie Waadia. She lives in the UK and runs a successful business with a worldwide reach. Pretty as a picture — inside and outside — Millie (that's the way we address her is in love with her Father, her Baba. Though thousands of miles apart, we came in contact with each other by Baba's kind grace. Our faith in His feet brought us together and wonderful are the relationships and bonds created by Him, for such divine connects are far more steadfast than any other relationships that man can ever build. Even though Millie and I have never met — at least not till the time when I started writing this experience — we are very close, very special friends. She has been more a soul sister to me, very affectionate and very dear.

This Incident dates back to a time when Millie was financially very well off and her career was at its prime. Her dedication and efforts were bearing sweet fruit. She had money, name, fame anci all that one could ask lor, when suddenly everything crashed. Her business went through a severe, unexpected downfall. Huge pecuniary losses overshadowed her peace. Kvery new morning only dawned to the devastating news of more losses, loans, bills and anguish. I remember those days, clear as crystal in my memories. Millie would work days at length with no rest, not even sleep. I always asked her where she derived the strength to manage without even blinking a restful eye and she would respond with positive vibrancy, "It's not me. It's Baba. His blessings keep me going."

With fulth and effort, she was slowly getting things around, when big, unanticipated trouble walked right up to her doorstep. It was the police. A dishonoured cheque had been handed, over to the cops. This was a criminal offence, as per the law, prevalent in her country. Millie had no wrong intentions and had not issued the cheque to deceive or cheat anyone. She had issued it in anticipation of some funds that she was expecting. I knew this all along and so 1 was the biggest testimony to her truth and her clear intentions but I was, at the same time, too far away to be of any help. The funds she was expecting got delayed due to circumstances beyond her control and, subsequently, the cheque she had issued was turned down by the bankers and was returned to her client unpaid. He was furious and without giving her a chance to explain her position, filed a case against her in the court of law. Despite Millie's clean intentions, she was, according to accepted norms, considered as having committed an unlawful act.

Millie, who was just about 30 year's of age, had a huge burden on her young shoulders. She had already been struggling to make ends meet and now, to make things worse, she was taken by the cops to the police station and questioned for hours at length. I remember talking to her that night when she finally got home and, to be honest, she didn't sound too good. She shared with me that while the cops did permit her to leave, they also gave her the date of 11 January, 2(106, which was about two-and-a-half months away. They informed her that during this period, a detailed enquiry would ho curried mil by them and if she was proved guilty, the result would In1 Imprisonment. ☺

One can well imagine what must have been her mental disposition at that moment. She was shattered, dejected and fearful. She did not want to worry her old parents, who lived in a different city and so she did not even share her woes with them. Everything had happened too suddenly. She wasn't aware of the enormity of her default, nor of any solutions to the problem.

She spoke to me, deep in thought, "I am not even sure what evidence can go against me and hold me guilty of fraud. I can't figure out any possible ways of getting out of this mess."

I offered my suggestions, howsoever useless they may have been, "Why don't you speak to the client who has filed the case against you and request him to be empathetic?"

"No, I can't do that," she replied. "The police have warned me not to interfere with their working and have specifically mentioned that ! must not get in touch with the client. That could create even more complications than I have on hand."

1 was quiet, sad and worried. But one thing I observed throughout these tough days was that though her mind was clouded by several doubts and uncertainties, her heart was as clear as a mirror. She knew deep in her heart that she had no wrong intentions of cheating her client and had got caught in this situation due to her misfortune and not due to her misdoings, and this gave her enormous strength.

When our eyes are misty and can't see the road ahead, our hearts lead the way — our hearts that are lit up by our faith in our Mother Sal. Millie was Baba's child and outwardly she did appear fragmented hut deep inside she was brewing with Baba's love. Situations were adverse but faith was strong.

"I am fine, I'uja," she said to me. "Baba is with me. 1 will not give up or give In. I am immediately starting a Saptah (weekly prayer) of Baba's *Satcharita* and I will keep doing *Saptahs* till Baba gets me out of this problem. I know that even if no one — be it friends or family — believes In mi1, baba knows the truth that I am not guilty."

She prayed to Mini, "Baba, please save me from imprisonment. And please get me out of this trouble without letting my name or my image get tarnished, Else, the after-effects of this case will ruin my business and my career forever. Please save me, Baba. You know my truth."

During the two-and-a-hall months that followed, she did several readings of the Satcharita week after week, with immense faith and infinite patience. 1 also advised her to mix ,i little of Baha's Udi in water and drink this Amrit first thing every morning. As [he days decreased in number, her faith increased in power. It is a fact that prayers make us stronger and calmer. Even science has accepted through research that meditation and prayers increase the levels of the 'happy hormones' in our body. So despite the big turbulent storm that encircled Millie, she sat calm and composed in its vortex, illumined by her unshakeablc faith in her Baba.

Finally, January 2006 dawned. It was on 5th January that she called me up. During my conversations with her over the last two months she had always sounded very brave and strong. But on this day, her voice told me that she was quite nervous and the reason was obvious: the fateful day of llth January was fiercely approaching.

The anxiety in her voice was almost palpable, "Puja, I have called to tell you that [am starting a final reading of the Sai Satcharita today and the seventh day, ie, the day of completion, will fall on llth January... tne day I have to report at the police station. 1 have complete faith in Baba, but to be honest with you, I am a little disturbed. So, 1 have told Baba that if He sees that all will be fine and I will not get Imprisoned, then I must complete the reading of the Satcharita within seven days. But if Baba foresees any unfortunate circumstances for me in the future, then 1 should not be able to finish my reading."

I sank back in my chair. What had she done in her anxiousness?? She had set up a precondition for herself and just in case she failed in completing the reading or was left with less time and more pages, she would get extremely distressed. I had seen her resolute and strong like a tigress all along. 1 didn't want to see her losing faith at the most crucial moments. But I said nothing of this to her. All 1 did was that I prayed along, like I had always done, but this time I was far more persistent with Baba. He just had to stand by her. We were leaving Him with no other options.

Shri Sai Satcharita (the abridged English version) has 260 pages in all. Millie started her reading as vowed. In the last 2-3 months, she had read the Satcharita several times and had always completed it in the stipulated seven days. But... well, this time things were different. Some problem or the other cropped up and despite desperate efforts, Millie couldn't read enough. Normally, we maintain an average of 38-40 pages each day. But Millie just couldn't do it and the load got heavier with each day. 1 prayed silently.

The morning of the llth finally dawned. She called me up. 1 was hoping for some good news on her progress, with the reading.

She spoke, unusually calm, "1 am yet to read 130 pages." "What!!" I exclaimed, "...half the Satcharita?"

"Yes, half the Satcharita to be completed today," she continued, still very calm, "You know, Puja, even on my most difficult and trying moments, I am peaceful at heart because I know that however big the problem, Baba will always be with me and will never leave me alone. I don't know whether I will be able to complete these 130 pages today, but ! know for sure that whatever will happen, will be His Divine Will. And, even if 1 do get arrested, I will accept it as His wish. He is my Father and He knows what is best for me. Then why should 1 fear?"

I smiled in blissful silence as I found myself at a loss for words. My heart knew instantly that such thoughts of abounding inner strength, in such adverse times, could only come from Baba's children. She was so right. His will, will be the best will!! Baba is so merciful. He becomes the strength of our mind, the power of our soul and the tranquillity of our heart, during testing times. I was still smiling... rny tigress was back!! ☺

Millie continued her reading with faith, with no thought of hunger or thirst. The day went by and she kept reading with patience and undeterred willpower. It was 4.45pm and Millie still had a lot to read. I forgot to mention that she had received a call a few days back from the cops asking her to report to the police station at 6pm sharp on the 11th. So, she halted her reading in order to get dressed and proceed for this final meeting. She closed her eyes in a final prayer before getting up: "I surrender myself in Your Holy Feet with complete trust, Baba. I shall accept whatever comes my way as Your wish, my Father's wish."

Just then the doorbell rang. Millie opened the door and was taken by surprise to find two policemen looking back at her. As she narrated to me later, "Puja, my heart almost stopped beating. My mind was clouded with questions. Why are they here? Are they here to arrest me? If they have come home, there has to be a reason big enough."

Fear took hold of her, and tears blurred her vision. "I recognized one of them. He was the officer-in-charge of my enquiry. He was the one, who had interrogated me very impolitely during our previous meeting. I looked at him with questioning eyes. He smiled back, surprisingly, and spoke rather politely, quite unlike our previous meeting.

"'Ma'am, we are here to inform you that you need not visit the police station today, as scheduled. We have not been able to collect any evidence against you. In fact, unexpectedly, the client who had filed the case against you has not been responding to our queries. He just doesn't appear interested in taking the case further. So we have decided to drop the charges against you.'

"Ohh!! Drop the charges??" exclaimed an astonished Millie.

"'Yes, Ma'am!! Drop Ihe charges. So, we came here to apprise you with these details. You can now relax at home. It is very cold outside and we did not want you to unnecessarily venture out in the snow. Sorry for the inconvenience caused. Goodnight.'"

Millie stood there; shocked, aghast. She stared in disbelief, as the two men walked away. Tears trickled down her cheeks as she stepped inside and stood before Baba's picture. He had not only saved her but had done so in such a magical way. Do cops walk up to the house of offenders and ask them to relax at home, as the weather outside is freezing? Do people who file cases not cooperate with the police for their own lost money? Is life so simple and so magical or is it our Big Magician working His magic upon us?☺ Well, obviously, we all know that with our kind-hearted Baba as our magician, life has to be magical. He pulls the strings and everyone simply dances to His tunes, be it the police or her client because with His grace even the Impossible becomes possible.

So, Millie did complete the stipulated 130 pages that day after the cops left and then cooked delicious sweets for dear Baba and revelled in the sunshine of His love. Her problem was very big in magnitude but her faith was bigger. I just pray to Baba that He blesses all His children with the same resilience and inner glow with which He blessed Millie. Because when our heart is radiating His love, no darkness can touch us. The miraculous powers of the Sai Satcharita proved to be infallible, yet again. And stronger still is the Power of Faith. If troubles manifest as darkness, our prayers and our faith manifest as divatyas, as candles, as effulgence. However dark the night is, the candle always makes a joyful difference.

Aum Sai Shri Sai faya Jaya Sai

Let the world go topsy-turvy, you remain where you are. Standing or staying in your own place, look on calmly at the show of all things passing before you. Demolish the wall of difference that separates you from Me; mnd then the road for our meeting will be clear and open. The sense of differentiation, as I and thou, is the barrier that keeps away the disciple from his Master-, and unless that is destroyed the state of union or atonement is not possible. 'Allah Malik' i.e., God is Supreme. His method of work is extraordinary, invaluable, and inscrutable. His will, will be done and He will show us the way, and satisfy our heart's desires. It is on account c/Rinanubandh [former relationship] that we have come together. Let us love and serve each other and be happy. He who attains the supreme goal of life is immortal and happy; all others merely exist., i.e., live so long as they breathe."

— SAI BABA OF SHIRDI

How Prayers Become Miracles ☺

"These feet are old and holy, you are cart-free now; place entire faith in Me and you will soon get your obfect."

Is your faith in Baba really strong and unbreakable or is it weak and fragile? Is your trust in His Holy Feet independent of the outcome of your expectations or is it conditional? Do you love Him wholeheartedly or is your love dependent on your needs, demands and wishes? Do you visit His temple only when you are in trouble or pain or do you run to meet Him all the time because you can't live without seeing His divine form? Is your devotion unfaltering, persistent and resolute or do you vacillate and swerve if He doesn't answer your prayers instantly? Look within, think and answer these questions with complete honesty because these answers will serve as a test of your faith and your love for your Sai,

A devotee once asked Baba, "Deva, there are so many who seek Your divine intervention to free them of their troubles and run to You in times of need. Do they all get the benefit of Your darxlsanl Are the prayers of all these devotees answered?"

To this Baba replied, smiling, "Look at the mango tree in blossom. If all the flowers become fruit, what a splendid crop it would be. But do they? Most fall off (either as flowers or as unripe fruits) by wind, storm, etc. Very few remain."

Are you one of those few who remain or one of those who give up their faith too soon? Let us first understand what Baba was trying to

explain by using the example of the mango tree and then answer this question.
When a mango tree is in full blossom, it bears innumerable flowers. The flowers that bloom on the tree have to face strong winds, downpours of rain and several other natural phenomenon. How long they can smile in gaiety perched up on the branches depends on how strong their bond is with the tree. Those with a weak connect fall off even with a light breeze. Only very few finally remain and become ripe fruits. So, of the uncountable flowers that had initially grown on the tree, only a handful of fruits survive till the end.

Similarly, a Stidgiiru such as Sai Baba has millions of devotees flocking to His Holy Feet, '['hey have a heart-to-heart bond with their Baba just like the flowers have a bond with the mango tree. These devotees with all their faith run to Baba in times of need. **But when devotion is merely need-based, it cannot be called true devotion. If faith is conditional, it is not faith at all. When our prayers are not accompanied by love and complete, absolute trust in His Holy Feet, they are not prayers but selfish desires.** And selfish desires obviously go unanswered because they are not from the heart and so fail to reach Baba's heart. So, when we pray to Baba but can't connect with Him in that prayer, the bond breaks and the devotees — just like the flowers — break away from the tree called Baba, and fall down.

We must also remember here, Baba's dictum, **"Tests will always be there. Those who have Nishtha (firm faith) and Saburi (infinite patience) shall qualify for My blessings."** So those that have undiluted faith and patience, accompanied by pure love and devotion are those that finally remain. And they survive through the vicious vortex of testing (imes because they derive their strength and courage from these words of advice: **'One huge unbearable problem in your life could be a small test that Baba is putting you through. And this small test could translate into your big opportunity of proving your unwavering faith in your Sai.'** Therefore, don't grow weak during testing times; grow stronger. And, at the same time, grow spiritually and let each problem take you a step close to your Lord, your Sai. He loves you unconditionally and all He wants from you in return is unconditional love; a love that is free of ifs and burs.

Baba's thirst for true devotion, unswerving faith and unfaltering perseverance is insatiable. The more you give Him, the more His thirst increases. Not only are we His dependents but He is dependent on His bhaktas too. He hungers only for our love. So give Him love in abundance. Let it overflow till He gets submerged head deep under it. And let not the flow stop even then because the more you give to Him, far more will you receive in return. What a beautiful and blissful life would it be — Baba flooded by our love and we, in turn, flooded by His love. 'I'his is the purest relationship in the universe — the relationship between a guru and his disciple. So let this love knock you off your feet. Flow in it, sink in it and finally get drowned in it because the deeper you go, the higher you will rise and the higher you rise, the closer you will get to your God, your Sai. Close your eyes and visualize — Sai submerged in your love and you submerged in His love. All around there is only love. There are no barriers, no walls, just you, your Sai and love. And all roads, all channels for your union with your God get opened... and in the end you finally merge in your Lord and become one with Him. Now there is no disciple, no guru... just one Supreme Atma, one Paraniattna.

My life has been sanctified by a series of miracles, visions, dreams and blessings. When I look back today, I realize what a major impact they have had on niy thought process, on my belief systems and on my life as a whole. I wish to share a deep learning that 1 have taken from these many events of my life; a learning that miracles are nothing but prayers offered with true conviction and belief. When we hear from friends or read about miraculous incidents, we are left in awe and bewilderment. Our heart believes and rejoices but our mind wishes to question their verity. For quite a period of my life I thought like this too. But today 1 am tempted to share my realization that miracles are as innate to us as our intuitive abilities. I use the word innate because no outside force triggers them. **Our faith, our belief and the power**

of our thoughts and prayers stimulate each and every miracle. If the strength of your mind (read thoughts), the conviction in your heart and the effulgence of your soul are weaved together in a single thread, the outcome is the instant gratification of what you prayed for or sought. And when we get what we want 'unexpectedly', we name it a miracle. The fact is that when our mind and heart reach the same depth and vibrational frequency as our Soul (read God), it synchronizes with the vibrational frequency of th(j, Universe (again, read God) and then all Cosmic Energies (read God, yet again), come together to give you what you wish for. So pray with faith and conviction and God will readily grant what you pray for. But remember, your prayer must have a lining of faith and not of doubt or disbelief.

I am going to narrate yet another miracle in my life to substantiate that honest prayers always end as miraculous gifts. I am taking you back to the time when 1 was barely four years old. Thanks to my saintly parents, I was growing up in the midst of a positive atmosphere illumined by virtuous teachings and inherent compassion. Needless to say, that as a child I was imbibing whatever was coming my way.

I always told my Maa and Paa that I wanted a little brother to play with. This request was seeded in the datum that most of my little friends had siblings. So 1 insisted that I wanted one as well. As narrated earlier, my parents had gone through so much trauma before 1 was born that they in no case wanted to risk another baby, especially for (he fear of having a boy. But tiny me had no clue about all this and so was persistent in my requests.

My helpless mother, tired of her obstinate daughter's daily tenacity, gave in one day and spoke, "My baby, let me explain to you. These things are not in our hands. Only God decides when He wants to send a baby to our home. And once He decides, then a stork brings the baby to us. So, it really won't help if you ask me for one. You must ask God to send you a baby brother or sister."

I looked at Maa with big eyes and some anger, "Why didn't you tell me earlier, Mamma? 1 would have asked Him for a brother long back and got one by now."
And then I had more questions, "But, Mamma, how do I ask Him for one?? Will He listen to me, if I speak? And are you sure He will give me what I ask for? What if He doesn't?"

Now this is where, in my most formative years, I learnt a lesson on praying from Maa. **"God is in your heart, my dear. Any prayer that you make to Him with love shall be granted for sure. But we must keep praying and not give up because God wants to see how honest and persistent our prayers are."**

Two things happened simultaneously. The first, Maa was relieved from the burden of my daily dose of questions and demands. And second, my next target, dear God, was going to be under tremendous pressure hereon. ☺

As Maa tells me now, she was so helpless before me that she had no option but to divert my attention elsewhere. And since she didn't want me to go after Dad, she veered my thoughts towards positive prayers anil God. Little did she know what she had done. © It is strange but 1 have crystal-clear memories of those days. I vividly recall, whenever Maa would play devotional songs at home — which was every day — I would sit right then, right there, on the carpet in our living room, hands folded, eyes closed and pray for hours at length. Initially, my parents thought it was so wonderful to see their little girl so prayerful. But I am also told that at times 1 caused social embarrassment, as 1 would sit with my eyes closed and start praying to devotional songs, played at just about any place, any time. And when people would question my intentions, I would innocently share that I was praying for a brother. I do smile today, at what my poor parents must have gone through back then.

Years went by and my prayers and determination grew stronger as I grew up. 1 started talking to God and speaking my heart out to Him.

(And Ibis habit continues even today.) Mamma's words from that conversation were etched in my heart: **"...we must keep praying and not give up because God wants to see how honest and persistent our prayers are."** Here was Baba's lesson of faith and patience, coming straight from my Mamma. So I prayed and prayed and prayed... with innocent and complete faith, and with loads and loads of perseverance.

God is kind, I always knew and believed. But that my parents were not party to my prayers, I did not know. They probably lacked the courage to go through another fearful nine months of pregnancy and childbirth, and 1 am sure my praying for 'a brother' must have made it worse for them, having known from doctors that a boy-child born to them would most likely not survive. So on one side my prayers continued unabated and on the other side was the firm and final decision of my parents of not having a baby (which I obviously wasn't aware of).

I was now eight years old. Dad was posted in the beautiful valley of Kashmir. Mamma was not keeping well. She was visiting doctors on a regular basis hut no one could figure out her ailment. She had even been treated for malaria and had to take quinine tablets (which I am told were so huge during those days that one could not even swallow them with ease). She had strange symptoms and no relief. Finally, Dad thought she should take a little vacation and a change of place would probably help. He couldn't get leave, so he booked Mamma and me on a flight to Delhi, from where we took a train to my maternal uncle's house in Kota (a city in Rajasthan). [was very excited to be with my cousins. We were meant to spend a fortnight with them. I was having a fun holiday but Maa was not getting any better. She was now being checked for typhoid.

In the meanwhile, I shared my desperation for a baby brother with my cousins. My older cousin reaffirmed my prayers by telling me thai in such cases, we should take oaths. So one night, as 1 lay in bed, i closed my eyes, prayed once again and did that too. I took a very severe oath as a little girl, an oath that "when I get my brother... I will do this and that." I apologize for not writing details of the 'this and that' but I had promised back then that these were secrets between God and me. All Ican say is that today I cannot do what I did back then. I am not capable of fulfilling such an austere oath now. It must have been God's blessing that 1 did what I did, back then.

The next morning is engraved in my heart; in fact, in my soul 1 should say. 1 woke up to bright sunshine in my eyes and I was ecstatic.

1 ran to my mum, "Mamma, God has heard my prayers." I was not speaking, 1 was screaming. I hugged her, "Mamma, last night God came in my dream. He was so bright and beautiful, wearing a long, white robe. He called me to Him and gave me a small baby in my arms," I recounted. "Mamma, He smiled and said, 'Here's your baby sister. Take her.' She was so tiny, Mamma. I held her tightly, close to me."

Right after saying this, I still recall breaking into thoughtful silence, "Ohhhh!! But, Mamma, He gave me a sister. Looks like He forgot that I was asking for a brother."

Mamma smiled back at me, looking very sick. She had apparently been barfing all morning. She dismissed my excitement as 'just a little girl's dream' (as she tells me now) but did give a warm, happy hug to keep my heart and also told me to be happy with whatever God gave me in my dream.

She fortified my faith that 'God's will is the best will' by her powerful words, "You should thank God for the little sister He tendered in your arms. So what if it is not a brother? At least He has given you a sister to play with. Vou must have faith that whatever He does must he the best for you."

I was satisfied with that explanation and then went on unstoppably, to share my dream with one and all.

Soon, Mamma left with my maternal aunt to visit the doctor. A lot of tests had been carried out in the last few days and her reports were expected that day. She reached the clinic, a little fearful of the unknown. She had been ill for 3-4 months now.

The doctor smiled, "Mrs Warn, congratulations. You are pregnant."

'Surprise, disbelief, astonishment' are the few words she uses to emote her first feelings. Joy, smiles and happiness set in a little later because this was totally unexpected, unplanned, I am told. Though there had been no signs of pregnancy all along, now the doctor informed her that she was already in the fourth month. Mamma ostensibly had no signs or symptoms of carrying a child. She had been pregnant four times before, but this time was so different. There was no single indication that she was bearing a baby in her womb.
She tells me with a huge smile even today, "My first thought on hearing the doctor's declaration, glided towards you. I smiled within my heart, thinking, 'Doctor, what my reports and tests have told you now, my little girl told me right in the morning. Strangely enough, she already knew it.'"

She smiles blushingly even today, "When 1 met your dad, on our return to Kashmir, his first statement was, 'Looks like your brother and bliabhi (his wife) have really looked after you well.' His gaze was on my tummy. When 1 told him that the tummy was more visible than before, not because I had been fed in excess, but because I had come back with a baby, he couldn't believe it too."

He says, "It took me a long time to come to terms with this news. We had been married for over 16 years. Your mother was 41 years of age. The Icasl we expected at this time was the news of a baby." They still smile and repeat a statement that I have very happily heard, by now, a million times, "This baby in our house is only due to your faith and prayers, Puja... totally your faith and noihing else."

And then, when the beautiful, blissful valley of Kashmir was enveloped by soft, white sheets of snow, the stork did finally pay us a visit. It was 9th September, Thursday (Sai Baba's day, who was then, not known to us physically but had connected with us spiritually) and it certainly was, is and shall remain the brightest morning of my life © — despite the cold snow — when I first held my little baby sister in my arms. Yes, a sister it was!! A recap of my dream happened; it truly did, when 1 hugged 'my bundle of joy' close to my heart, in my tiny arms. And Neha, as we affectionately refer to her, has been the greatest joy in our lives. She has been more my daughter, less my sister. We are bonded by far deeper karmic connections, than the mind can possibly envisage. Needless to mention that true to my promise made to God, I did fulfil the oath 1 had taken before her birth.

Neha's celestial entry was far more than the coming of a little sibling in my life. Without bearing a child in my womb, I experienced the divinity of motherhood, all thanks to her. And not just that, she was an answer to my prayers. Her coming marked a new chapter in my spiritual journey. At a very raw age, I realized and accepted an unsaid truth: that I could get whatever I deeply and truly desired in this life through honest, persistent prayers. Neha's birth was to the world 'a miracle' caused by 'divine intervention'. To me, it was a reaffirmation of my faith in the indisputable 'power of prayer'. This brings to an end, my happy story and at the same time, hopefully, marks the beginning of a lire illumined by faith and prayer, for the readers. 1 am certain that **'anything aspired for, with unblemished faith and fervent prayers, bears fruit'. Prayers are like yeast; they take some time to swell up but once they do, they act as catalysts to a life of fulfilment and bliss.**

Aum Sai Shri Sai Jaya Jaya Sai

"The teachings of a, Guru are of no use to a man who is full of egoism and who always thinks about the sense-objects. Purification of mind is Absolutely necessary; without it., all our spiritual endeavours are nothing, but useless show and pomp. It is, therefore, better for one to take only what he can digest and assimilate. My treasury is full, and I can give anyone what he wants, but I have to see whether he is qualified to receive My gift. If you listen to Me carefully, you will be certainly benefited. Sitting in this Masjid, I never speak any untruth."

— SAI BABA OF SHIRDI

When Gun Shots could not Kill...

Doubts and difficulties surround us fust to move us and confirm our faith. We are tested as it were. If we only hold on steadily toBaba with full faith and continue our endeavours, our efforts will be ultimately crowned with success.

Baba to us is Brahma, Vishnu, Mahesh (Trimurti Incarnate) — the Creator, the Preserver and the Destroyer, respectively. He is Jesus, He is Allah, He is Nanak, He is the Lord Almighty. Guru is God.... Those who see any difference between them are yet embryonic and unripe. To us, Baba, our Gum, is no different from God. He created the beautiful universe. Mountains, valleys, oceans and rivers, all originated from Him. He made the sunshine brighten our days and the moonlight did away with our dark nights. He gave life to all His creations. Each plant, each animal breathes His love. And so, all His creations have one thing that binds them together: His Soul, His Atrna. Yes, from the tiniest ant to the mightiest mountain, all have a Universal Soul in common. Have you ever thought why is it that when we are happy, nature seems happy too and when we are sad, it feels as though gloom is cast over our entire world? This happens because the Universal Soul rests in all of nature and in each one of us too. Nature feels what we feel and vice versa. Such is the beauty of being a part of the Cosmic Oneness, a part of the Cosmic Soul.

This magnificent universe, created by our God, is His biggest miracie in itself. All other miracles look so small, so inconsequential when we compare them with His timeless, boundless creation: the marvellous universe. Human beings are perhaps the next most enthralling work of our mighty, opulent Lord because He bestowed upon us the special faculty of 'thought'. He wanted us to appreciate His work and so gave us the power to think. But this also meant that now, our deeds — our karmas — came to depend entirely on us because we were blessed with the inborn ability 'to think', 'to decide' and 'to choose' between what is right and what is wrong. We were expected to take our decisions but we proved incapable of doing so. We mostly endecLup in a dilemma and could not decide what to choose, which way to go. God solved that problem, too. When He created this beautiful universe, He Himself could have lived anywhere and in any place that He desired: every bit of this universe belonged to Him. But He too needed a permanent abode, a place where He could rest and be comfortable. He could have lived in the clouds or made a glorious palace in the midst of the stars. He could have even created a city under the vast ocean or built a castle in the endless blue sky. But He was so kind, so benevolent and loved us so much that He gave up all those beautifu! dwellings and instead chose to live in our heart. This was His special way of telling us that He loved us and cared enormously for us.

So, now He resides within each one of us as our Guiding Light. He speaks only the truth and nothing but the truth. His answer is always the best answer to our questions, our doubts and our dilemma. So, in life whenever we are unsure of our decision or in fact even if we are sure, the best way would undoubtedly be His way. **Sit quietly, in peace and then speak to Baba, who is your Inner Voice. Ask Him the question that is troubling you or making you restless and trust Him completely, for His Solution will certainly be the Best Solution; His Path will definitely he the Best Path. You will hear Him speak from within your heart and bless you with such unimaginable answers that you yourself could have never thought of, answers that only He can give.**

Baba says, "Look within. Know Me. Recognize Me as the One who is seated in your heart. I am your Inner Voice. Hear Me speak. Trust Me completely. And 1 will give direction to your life and guide you safely along its difficult path." So have faith in His words and learn to trust the voice of your heart, which is nothing else but His pure voice. **Don't run after outward happiness**

because happiness lies within. True happiness is where your heart is, and your heart is where Baba is. So our happiness is where our Sai is. ☺

1 must narrate here an incident that relates to the Raina family. This is something that will certainly send shivers down your spine and make you hold your breath in amazement. Never before have I come across such a story of Baba's Divine Intervention. Gunshots, terrorists, houses ablaze... it has all the elements of a blockbuster film. But the only difference is that films are fictional, whereas this is a real-life incident.

The Raina family belongs to the beautiful, picturesque valley of Kashmir. Nature blessed Kashmir to be 'the heaven on earth' but unfortunately man-made religious biases and hatred made it worse than hell. We have just read how the entire nature belongs to God but we human beings even divided His universe, His world and His land into mine and yours. We created boundaries and today we suffer totally because of our own doings. A war continues in Kashmir for uncountable years, a war to possess a piece of land. No one realizes that it is God's world and His land. We are here today, we shall be gone tomorrow... our lives are subject to birth and death. But all of nature was always God's nature and shall stay His nature till eternity. Still, in the few years that we live, we fight over a portion of land that was never ours and that shall never be ours. We draw borders and lines of control, not realizing that dividing God's world is completely beyond our control.

Back now to the Rainas, who lived in Kashmir during the most turbulent times; times when there was bloodshed and war; times when self-professed men of God decided to burn the Kashmir! Pandits alive it they refused to leave Kashmir; times when a fanatic sect of people wished to possess God's Kashmir.

It was a Sunday, when three terrorists approached the huge bungalow that belonged to the Rainas. Several of their relatives and friends had left their ancestral homes and age-old attachments and fled from Kashmir due to the havoc and fear created by terrorism that had become endemic to Kashmir and had eaten through its roots. Now the terrorists were specifically picking on those people who had stood their ground and decided not to leave their entire world behind and flee. The Rainas were one of them.

The terrorists entered their driveway and broke all glass doors and towering windows using the stubs of their rifles and AK-47s. It was a regular feature to first traumatize and harass the residents and then shoot them.

In the words of Sheetal, their daughter, "One of the three stayed at the main gate and the other two stomped inside the house. They then broke the main door, whilst Mummy and Papa locked themselves in one of the bedrooms, where we had a big photo of Bahaji. They felt somewhat secure to have Baba with them. Mummy had hidden my young cousin who was staying with us, under the bed, rolled in a carpet, behind the gas cylinders, in the other room. I was, on this fatehil clay, at the same cousin's house, in Delhi. My parents had sent me there, so that I would be taken care of, if something happened to them."

Sheetal's voice trembled as she went on, "The two terrorists kept banging on the bedroom door. My parents were worried that in case they didn't open the door, the terrorists may trace my young cousin in the other room or even set the entire house ablaze. So out of sheer helplessness, Mummy opened the door."

I must share here that Mrs Raina is a stocky woman with a huge built and is vibrant and full of life. She is famously known as Bengashi (elder sister, in the Kashmiri folklore) amongst all who know her. She is a woman of enormous inner strength and immense physical power. On the contrary, her husband, Mr Raina, is a lean, slender-looking man, very soft-spoken, tender and frail. They love Baba and swear by His love and presence in their lives.

Getting back to Sheetal's narration, "Chanting Babii's name and praying for grace, Mummy opened the door and asked the terrorists what they wanted and why they were breaking Into our house. They didn't reply. Instead, one of them asked ihe other to shoot my mum; that is what they did in most cases. But I think Baba had something else in mind. For some strange reason — Jai Sal Ram — his gun got stuck on his shoulder!!!! He pulled at his gun but It |ust wouldn't come off. So, the other one, instead, dragged Mummy to the living room and mercilessly pushed her there. In the confusion, her head hit the sofa and she fainted."

At this Sheetal paused, teary eyed and my heart took a pause too. I was left to wonder, had the gun not got stuck at the right time, I would have never got to meet this wonderful daughter of Baba, called Bengashi. Her call of love to her Father had saved her life, this once. But what next, I wondered, and looked at Sheetal with questioning eyes.

She continued, "Whilst he was locking the room with Mummy inside, the other terrorist had his gun pointed at Papa. Right in front of Papa was the terrorist and behind him was Baba's huge picture. As Papa looked at the picture one last time, thinking it was his end, he suddenly felt as though he was being bathed by a ray of bright, radiant light coming straight from Baba. In a matter of seconds, I'apa got this sudden, colossal power to fight back the terrorists. He is just not one of those who can fight... Jai Sai Ram!!!!!" she smiled.

I loved the way each of Sheetal's 'life-saving' sentences, ended in a Jai Sai Ram. ☺

My smile was very momentary. 1 gasped when she continued, "Papa was hit by two bullets on his right shoulder, while fighting them. They were very well built and were two against one. Papa was frail; they thought he was alone. Little did they know that Papa had dear Baba by his side, With two bullets in his shoulder, he fought on with an 'other-worldly' power. It was certainly Baba who fought. To the terrorists' eyes it was Papa fighting, but we know — our hearts know — and even Papa knew that it was Baba fighting. It was totally Divine

Intervention. Papa fought back till the end and even, almost killed one of the two terrorists. Finally, when they had exhausted all their bullets, they ran from the house to bring back some more of their people. In the meanwhile, all wounded and bleeding profusely, Papa opened the room in which Mummy had been locked. Sh* had, by then, fortunately regained consciousness. She cried out at the sight of Papa, soaked in blood."

1 felt sorry, to have asked Sheetal to narrate this incident to me. I was guilty of her pain, her tears and of bringing back all her agonizing memories. But the sweet girl went on, despite her hurt, so that this story of Baba's love could reach all of us, His children.

"Mummy cried in despair. She knew no one would dare help us because if they did, they would be the next easy targets for the terrorists. Papa was bleeding and there was no way they could reach the hospital. She rushed back to Baba's picture and begged Him to save Papa's life. He had saved them till now and she believed that He would again come to their rescue. And He did!! After about 15-20 minutes, an auto-rickshaw driver came to the main gate of the house to deliver a gas cylinder. But it was a Sunday... a holiday... and everyone knew that the agency would be closed. So it was liabaji, who sent him to save my parents. Despite the risk to his own life, he took them to a nearby hospital.

"In the meantime, the terrorists returned and found out where my parents had gone. They couldn't break into the hospital. They were so furious and so full of vengeance that they got hold of a doctor from their own sect and compelled him to inject poison into Papa. Papa was critical by then and Mummy was sitting by his side chanting Baba's name. Imagine the grace of Baba; as the doctor was about to inject my dad, my mother just had a strong feeling, as though Baba was upset and disturbed and was asking her to be cautious, that something was not all right. She jumped up from her seat and stopped the doctor and asked him to first carry out some sort of a sample check, before injecting Papa. The doctor refused and from his strange behaviour Mum understood that something dubious was going on in the hospital. She threatened the doctor, crying aloud that if anything happened to her husband, she would burn their hospital. Poor Mummy was seeing Papa bleed out before her very eyes and no medical help was coming. All she could do was pray and she again beseeched Baba's blessings. Suddenly, from somewhere a Sardar (Sikh) doctor walked in. He spoke to Mummy very kindly, addressing her as 'sister'. He requested her to calm down and promised to do everything possible to save Papa. He then carried out a surgery and finally got the bullets out of my dad's shoulder." Sheetal smiled in relief, as though the bullets had just been removed.

Then she went on, "In the meanwhile, the police came to our house and from there to the hospital. They told Mum that it was not safe for them to go back home and it would be better If they left Kashmir right then, as the terrorists had gathered in huge numbers and were on a lookout for them to return. One of the senior police officials booked the tickets for Mummy, Papa and my cousin, and straight from the hospital they went to the airport, still In their nightdothes and finally landed in Delhi. We came to know later that the terrorists took out the brand-new clothes that Mummy had kept aside tor my wedding, hung them on trees and burnt them. After burning our belongings publicly, they set our house ablaze to vent their anger and frustration. But with Baba's grace, my parents were now no more in that house. Baba had appeared in different forms all along and saved their lives."

What more can I add to this tale of a thousand miracles and blessings?

Sheetal's mum said to me with a very 'all-knowing' look of deep faith, "It was Baba, again and again. He first saved my life by getting the gun stuck in the terrorist's shoulder. Then His eyes, powerful as thunderbolt, electrified my husband with a strength he had never known before. He always says that it was Baba within him who fought back the weapon-laden terrorists. Where would my timid, soft husband have the power to fight two huge men, that too with two gun shots in his shoulder? Then again, Baba came to us as the auto-rickshaw driver and escorted us to the hospital. And finally He saved my husband's life as the Sikh doctor. We saw death face to face again and again, yet we escaped it... only because of our Baba Sai."

This is what faith in Baha does to people. I am in awe, admiration and am lost for words, as usual. He comes to us in one form or the other but He comes for sure. Anyone who keeps undying faith has to he rescued, whatever the situation. We, the children of Sai, are indeed fortunate. We don't have to rely on people or worldly situations for help. We don't have to run from pillar to post in helplessness or despair. We only have to chant His a 11-purifying, energizing name and pray for His grace... and then and there His Magic begins. ☺

Aum Sai Sliri Sai Jaya Jaya Sai

"Ah, he says that I fn-amised him to come hut deceived him. Inform him that I did attend his dinner, but he failed to recognize Me. Then wlty did he call Me at all'? See, to keep My words / mmld sacrifice My life, I would never be untrue in My words."

— SAI BABA OF SHIRDI

Maa, Two Rotis Please!

Baba said, "Did you not hear My words? It was no vision but direct order. My words are always pregnant with meaning and never hollow."

When i sit down to pray... my Guru, my Baba becomes 'Light'... He assumes the form of a tliya... a 'candle'.... When I read the Holy Gita... He becomes Krishna... when I hear a discourse on the Ramayana... He becomes Ram... when 1 hold the Holy Bible... He becomes Christ... when I visit thegitnulwara... He becomes Nanak... and when I open the Holy Quran... He becomes Allah.

My Guru is so wonderful... He is always with me... at every moment... in every breath. When I cry in pain, He becomes my tears; when I smile in joy, He becomes my happiness; when I feed a poor child, He becomes the sacred food; when I clothe the naked, He becomes the warmth wrapping up the cold body; when 1 read, He becomes knowledge; and when 1 write, He becomes my words.

Overwhelming is the love of our Guru, Sai Baba. It is like taking a dip in the ocean and getting the blessings of all the sacred rivers that have poured themselves into its holy waters. It is like battling in the sunshine of His warmth and soaking in the showers of His affection... all at once. It changes the way we perceive life, it changes our inner core. It makes us better human beings; it makes us caring, sharing and compassionate. 1'ain loses its prick and no storm, however turbulent, disturbs us, our lives or our wortd. Baba's love makes our heart calm as a lake and our world full of bliss and peace. **We, Baba's children live Ihc lives of Yogis... nothing unsettles our minds; in pain we are calm, in joy we are composed. We drink through His eyes... the ambrosia of Divine Love... and we are left cleansed, purified and sanctified.** Such is the love and the grace of our Guni, our Baba.

Baba's love is unique and so are His methods of imparting wisdom or sharing love. Sometimes He gives us messages and hints to help and guide us, sometimes He answers our queslions through His Satcharita; at times He comes to meet us as an old man and at other times in any nmp, any fonan. And on some beautiful occasions He comes in our dreams to bless us or to share with us important teachings. Inscrutable are His ways and innumerable are His approaches. But the aim is one... to stand by us through good and bad, night and day, joy and sorrow.

[n 1917, one year prior to Baba's MahasamatIM, He appeared In His devotee Hemadparit's dream, one festive morning, dressed as a sanyasi. Hemadpant is the blessed soul who has written the invaluable Sa! Satcharita. In the dream, Baba appeared before him and spoke to him lovingly, "I will visit your house for meals today."

Hemadpant was happily surprised and told his wife about the dream. She was delighted to know this and cooked with love for Baba, wondering, at the same time, if He would come to have their coarse food at Bombay, leaving the delicacies cooked by His devotees at Shirdi. Then, at noon, when lunch was being served, the entire family waited with compiete faith and did not start eating In anticipation of Baba visiting them, though not knowing how and in what form their Sai would appear. But they had complete faith that Haba would fulfil the words spoken in Hemadpant's dream. If He said He would come, He surely would. So the whole family waited with love and faith and, right on time for lunch, two guests walked in, unexpected: Ali Mohammad and Moulana Ismu Mujavar. They apologized for disturbing the family during meals ami quickly presented to Hemadpant a huge package, wrapped In a newspaper cover, and then left. When Hemadpant eagerly unwrapped the parcel, his heart jumped in joyful ecstasy, as in his hand was his Baba, who had appeared in the form uf a beautiful picture to bless him. True to His word, Baba reached on time for lunch, in the form of a huge life-size portrait and fulfilled the promise made to Hemadpant in his dream.

The picture was placed on the centre seat reserved for the head of the fliimlly and Baba was offered food with lots of love and gaiety, after which the family partook of its meals.

Ninety years later, in 2007, Baba felt hungry for home-made food once again. © So, He once again appeared in an early morning dream; not as a sanyasi this time but as a fakir who wore a kafhi. The person who saw the dream after those ninety years was not Hemadpant who wrote the Stiri Sai Satcharita but it was me, who is penning down another blessing very similar to the Holy Sai Satcharita. ☺ The day was not special due to a festival, but was special as I had decided to begin on that day, a Saptah of my Satcharita reading,

Here's my dream... I was standing on the steps of a staircase leading to my house and at a little distance from me, In an open field, stood my sister Neha. We suddenly observed an old man, dressed in a kafiii, a cloth tied around Mis head, walking towards us. Neha and I exchanged glances wondering who this old man was, as He looked so similar to our Baba. While we were still wondering, He walked closer and sat down in the dusly field somewhere between the two of us. As we looked on, still unsim1 of His Identity, He sent a thrill down our spines when Hi' siit down In the posture similar to His Dwarkamai pictures. Neha and I once again exchanged glances in the dream but this time our eyes were shining with excitement, as our hearts had recognized the elderly fakir to be none other than our dearest Baba Sai.

But before we could react, He turned towards me and stretched out His arm. Then with His forefinger and middle finger, raised together in a 'V' sign, which symbolically appeared like two, He said to me, "Maa, can I get two rolls, please?"

His calling me 'Maa' reaffirmed my faith that il was none other than my Baba who was asking for rotis in my dream, us Baba always addressed women as Maa, Mai, etc, So I rushed up the steps of my house, excited and elated, to get the rotis, But, alas! At that moment, 1 was woken up by my doorbell and the dream ended.

When I woke up, I clearly remembered every small detail of my dream. I was truly overjoyed to have had a beautiful tlarshan of Baba. At the same time, 1 was unsure as to how to feed Him and fulfil His wish of the two rotis asked for in my dream. After contemplating for a while, I decided to cook something delicious, along with the two rotis and offer it to any old person, outside Baba's temple — as that was the only likely way of fulfilling Baba's wish.

1 knew that Baba was very fond of a dish called Kacharya. I had never cooked Kacharya in my entire life, so I read the details mentioned in the Sai Satcliaritu and accordingly cooked the dish, made up of round slices of brinjal fried in ghee, along with another nice dish. After this 1 sat down to pray and started my proposed Satchtirlta path (ritualistic prayer). 1 spent a long time reading and when I got up, It was almost 1pm and time for lunch.

I was quite exhausted by now and hungry too, as I had not eaten anything all morning. I wanted to first feed Baba and then eat, but now it was late and with family commitments, It was not possible for me to visit the temple right then. So, with a heavy heart, 1 decided to visit Baba's temple in the evening to feed an old man. But all along, 1 kept feeling very sad. I was really upset and kept thinking, how wonderful it would be if Baba could come to my door too, just as He had come in my dream and have fresh, warm hind for lunch. But unfortunately, I lived in an apartment and security was very high within the premises. No one could enter the gated society without genuine reason and identity check calls being made to the housemates. And I was not even expecting any visitors, who amid have probably come, with a gift of Baba's picture tor mi-, as had happened in Hemadpant's case. ☺ So, sad and detected, I brai'ed myself to wait till the evening and have no expectations whatsoever. My helpless eyes were still looking at Baba's picture and praying earnestly. But then 1 had to go on and finish cooking for the family, With a sad heart, 1 decided to start kneading the dough, something that 1 never did on other days. But this was a special day, as I had to serve Baba, so I was doing everything with my own hands, for the love of my Sai.

Tins-tons, tlng-tong... my doorbell rang twice. It was about 1.15pm. I was |ust starling to knead the dough. Wondering who it could be, I opened the door. A young boy around 14-15 years of age, dressed ml her poorly, was standing outside.

I looked at him, still wondering who he was, but before 1 could ask him anything, he spoke up instead. "Madam, can 1 get two rotis and some vegetable, please??" 1 stared at him in disbelief.

My heart was pounding. Honestly, I didn't know how to react. I was blank, completely sensation I ess. I just looked at him and, in a quivering voice, I responded, "Please wait! Stay right here. I'll get the food for you."

Tears overflowing and every cell of my being vibrating wildly, I ran back inside. With trembling hands and blinded eyes, 1 quickly kneaded the dough, prepared the two rotis and heated up the vegetables. Then with the food ready, I stood before Baba's picture and with loud sobs and tears of gratitude, I offered it to Him. Then finally I ran to the door, where the little boy was still waiting and handed over the food to him. He smiled a bright happy smile and his eyes lit up, at the sight of the food.

"Who are you?" I asked, now that I had calmed down slightly.

He replied with a shy smile, "I work in the apartments, as a sweeper."
I continued, "And how is it that you came to my house for food? I have been staying here for almost five years now and no one has ever come asking for anything."

At this he smiled yet again, "I was hungry, so I came."

Saying this he walked away with his two rotis and left me stunned and lost. ☺

1 don't know how to explain my feelings. Who was that boy? Where did he come from? Why did he come to my house, when there were over a hundred other houses In the vicinity? Why did he ask for two rotis only? Why did I never see him again? Who wai, he, for heaven's sake? To me, He was Baba, none other than my Baba. I had failed to recognize Him once before but this time I would not get deceived. Has not Baba promised that He would cross the seven seas to keep His word? He has always fulfilled His promises; He fulfilled His promises made in Hemadpant's dream as well as In mine and He will continue to do so, till eternity. He blessed me on that auspicious day. It was probably His unique way of expressing the golden emotions of love. Or maybe He was craving for Kacharya? He alone knows what He does and why. But we love it, don't we?

Baba has said in the Satcharita, **"I am dependent on him, who thinks and hungers after Me and who does not eat anything, without first offering it to Me. He who thus comes to Me, becomes one with Me, just as a river gets to the sea merges in it."** Maybe Haba was happy with my service of love, because I never even drink a sip of water without first offering it to Him or taking His name. Is Haha not always with us? We must offer Him first, before we partake of any food. Not only food, but also every feeling, every emotion, every profit, every loss, every joy, every sorrow, everything that we possess, must be offered unto His Holy Feet before it reaches us. And if our offering is humble and pure, He will surely accept it. Imagine how beautiful life would be, when we share all that we have with our very own liaba. **Food will become more delicious, clothes will suit us better, profits Will bring us more joy and sorrows will lose their sting. Therefore, let us love Baba, the way He dearly loves us. There is no difference between a Guru and His disciple. To the worldly eye, they appear as two bodies but they are in essence One Soul.**

Aum Sat Shri Sai Jaya Jaya Sai

*"What is the matter with you ? Why are you so turbulent? How is it that you are so quarrelsome? Can you not speak soft and sweet words? You read daily sacred books and still your mind is impure and your passions uncontrolled. What sort of a human are you ? TOM ought to be indifferent to mil things. A good human being should have no 'mamata1 [attachment] but have *samata' [equality] towards all."*

— SAI BABA OF SHIRDI

The Divine Magic Continues

Babaji said, "You destroy the wall between us, so that we can see and meet each otherface to face."

Baba, despite being God incarnate, never saw any difference between Himself and His children. He taught us the true lesson of Oneness. He, the Cosmic Soul, the All-powerful God Almighty, called Himself the servant, the slave of His people. He had no pride, no ego, not even a speck of it. He never showed-off His knowledge or flaunted His greatness. He was as simple as simplicity itself.

Once, a self-professed guru called Jwahar AM came to Shlrdi and claimed himself as Baba's guru. Baba did not feel the least disconcerted at this and even served him in various ways, just as a true sliishya would. Later, when Jwahar Ali realized Baba's true worth, he felt abashed and fell at Baba's feet for mercy. But our soft-hearted Baba did not feel bad at the treatment meted out to Him earlier. **He who could command the whole universe, all of nature with a mere movement of His hand or the slightest blinking of His eyes... He served as a disciple, and lived in noblest humility. And the Irony is that we, who have no worth before Baba... we, who art.- not even worthy of being compared to Him... live with a puffed-up, huge ego. What is our worth after all?**

If God can be so humble, why can't we? He created this universe, the mountains, the valleys, the rivers, plants, animals and humans... and He has no ego, not the slightest trace of it. And what are we proud of? A noble soul is one that lives sans ego and follows the exemplary conduct demonstrated by Baba. To secure Baba's eternal love, we must let go of our ego, our pride. We must stay away from arguments, disputes and disagreements. Baba says that those that argue have very strong 'Body Consciousness'. We must practise to be 'Soul Conscious' and the ego shall, by itself, die away slowly.

Baba's love is like a gem and only a gemmologist can know its worth or value. Those that read about Baba, without faith and with doubts and apprehensions, shall get the benefit of reading fiction or fables. But those that know the value of the priceless gem called Sai shall benefit in innumerable, uncountable ways. So let us rid ourselves of our alter egos, let us realize our soulful existence and then the wall that stops us from merging in our Baba shall turn to ashes and Divine Sublime Oneness shall remain.

But let me go back to sharing a few more stories of Baba's unconditional love and support to His children, and take you once again on a journey with Baba: partaking meaningful, lesson-full experiences, under the guidance and all-pervading eye of our Sadguru Sainath.

I have a maid called Soni, who has been working in my house for over three years now. She hails from a small village, where her parents married her off when she was barely 14. Soni is now just about 25 years of age and has three children, all daughters, aged eight years, five years and three years, respectively. Unfortunately, in Indian villages, the trend of child marriage continues unplugged. The age-old custom of marrying off a daughter early, which is followed by a series of pregnancies, at a very early age, has been a curse for her and several others. It has left her physically and emotionally very weak. Soni's youngest daughter, Aaliya, unfortunately had to bear the brunt of her debility. She suffered from a congenital disorder: her legs were lifeless. She was born that way. © The lower portion of her body did not react to touch. Doctors attributed this to excessive weakness in the mother's body, when Aaliya was in the womb. The little baby would not be able to take her body weight on her tiny feet, all throughout her iife. How I wish that parents who regard their daughters as burdens and get them married at a raw, unripe age, realize the damage they are causing to not only their daughter, but also their grandchildren.

When Soni started working in my house, Aaliya was not even one. As she grew up, it became apparent that the little girl would never walk and would have to live the rest of her life, minus her legs. This was not all, as another misfortune added to the woe of the parents: Aaliya could not speak: the baby was dumb as well as lame. It pains my heart to even imagine what agony it must have been for her parents — a pretty little girl, who could not move from one place to another, who could not even convey her feelings or even her barest needs. She was almost like another piece of furniture in their house.

Soni was a very simple, pure-hearted girl and was very close to my heart. One day, she suddenly broke down in front of me and wept profusely. She was really concerned about Aaliya, yet blatantly helpless. She was too poor to organize any medical help or treatment for the little girl. 1 too was in despair and felt hopeless. I sat pondering over options, ways and means of helping her out. I was considering speaking to my husband and working out some medical treatment for the baby, when my eyes suddenly fell upon Baba's smiling face in the portrait, right before my eyes, on the wall in front. Something strange happened; Baba's gaze pierced through me. I felt as though Baba's eyes were penetrating right into my heart. I could feel gooseflesh and at the very next moment, I had my answers. ☺

1 smiled back at Baba, got up from my seat, walked towards His picture and picked up a packet of Udi from there. Then I spoke to Soni, "Take this, my dear. **This is Baba's sacred Udi. It has worked wonders for those who have accepted it with faith and has cured even fatal diseases. So, you too have faith in Itaba. He will not let you down.** Give Aaliya a little Udi dissolved in half a bowl of water as holy Tirth (sacred water) and apply some of it to her forehead as well as her legs, every day. Baba will not only make her walk but also make her run one day. And I am sure, very soon, by the grace of Baba, she will not only speak but call out to you, her mama,

in her sweet voice. Stop crying and have faith.- Urust In Baba and trust in my words too. All will be well."

Saying this, 1 placed the Udi in Sorii's hands. She immediately closed her eyes, appeared to make a silent prayer and then, looking at Baba'* picture with her tearful eyes, wept on and on. After some time, she calmed down and then promised me that she would religiously do as told.

Time went by and I did ask her on 4-5 different occasions, whether she was following the Udi regimen as advised by me. But hei answers were ambiguous and unconvincing. I figured out that barring the first few days, she was not regular any longer. I decided not to compel her, as faith can never be imposed.

Seven to eight months went by. It was the day of Ashtami (a Hindu ritual), on the completion of Navratras (Nine Sacred Days). It was customary for our family to invite little girls on the day of Ashttimi for the puja ceremony. On this auspicious day, little girls are equated with Goddess Durga and worshipped with traditional customs and rites. Their feet are washed, they are duly worshipped and then offerings of food, gifts and money are made to them.

On this particular occasion, too, we as a family, were preparing to do the same. I beckoned the invited girls towards the terrace and washed their tiny feet, one after the other. The last little girl, who appeared to be (he youngest of the lot, excitedly ran towards me and with a shy smile said, "Didi, it is my turn now. Please wash my feet."

1 had never seen her before. She was cute, chubby and dark complexioned. 1 smiled back and asked aloud, "Whose daughter is she?"

1'at came the reply from inside the house, "Mine, Didi."

I looked up in disbelief, because I knew the voice: it was Soni's. I had asked her to bring her daughters over as well. And I very well recognized both her elder daughters. Then who was this little girl?

"Who is she, Soni?" I asked, still wondering; a motley of questions thundering through my head.

Soni smiled, "She is Aaliya, Ditii."

Aaliya... little Aaliya who could not even stand on her two tiny feet had just run towards me? The little girl who could not speak had just spoken with sugary sweetness to me? Was all this a dream? I again looked at Soni and 1 assume she read the surprise in my eyes.

"Didi, do you remember that several months back you had given me Babaji's Udi?"

1 nodded in affirmation, as she went on, "I applied the Udi on Aaliya's legs and feet for a few days and sometimes gave the Udi mixed in a spoon of water to her for drinking. 1 prayed to Baba to make Aaliya walk as well as talk and He always smiled back from Hi5 picture — the small one you gave me. I'll be honest with you that I was not regular. But during the initial days of application of the Udi itself, Aaliya's legs started moving. And over the next few months, she first slowly stood on her feet and then started walking. While her legs were gaining vitality, one day she suddenly looked at me and said, 'Maa'. And very soon she was not only walking hut also talking. We were very happy. Thank you, Didill 1 am sorry that I did not mention all this to you earlier."

I was shell-shocked. I genuinely did not know, whether I should have screamed aloud in anger at Soni that she had not bothered to share such overwhelming news with me or whether I should have screamed aloud in joy and ecstasy, at this heart- warming miracle of dear Baba. Rut as usual, I was left spellbound. Little Aaliya had started speaking and I had no words to speak! Ah Baba!! Only You know Your ways. You blessed the little girl with the Voice of Your love and I, Your little girl, had lost my voice, all thanks to the same love. ☺

I honestly don't have enough words to sing Your praise, Baba. You have taught me a glorious lesson in Your inimitable way. A hundred prayers, a million tears are not always needed. One honest prayer, tew tears of love and the impossible becomes possible. The lame begins to run, the blind awakens to see, the dumb starts to speak; such is the magic of Your Holy Udi and Your love. Thanks Baba, for blessing us with this Sublime Udi: Your Divine Remedy for all our mental, physical and material afflictions.

Aum Sai Shri Sai Jaya Jaya Sai

"You must bear the fruit — good or bud — of your past actions; if it is incomplete, suicide won't help you. Ton have to take another birth and suffer again; so instead of killing yourself, why not suffer for some time and finish up the fruit of your past deeds and be done with it once and for

— SAI BABA OF SHIRDI

The Rice Sacrifice

Baba often said, "He who carps and cavils at others, pierces Me in the heart and injures Me, but he that suffers and endures, pleases Me the most."

Life as we all know is like a curve with all its ups and downs. Happiness and sorrow, success and failure, pleasure and pain, and acceptance and rejection are all an essential part of this curve. Life can never be like a straight line which begins in happiness and ends in it as well. Despite this, whenever we are overcome by troubles, we react rather foolishly. Bad health, accident, theft, discord at home, tension at work, financial loss, emotional trauma... all leave us shattered. It is a well-known fact that life minus suffering is nothing but a dream. Still we lose our inner strength and poise and in most cases start hurling allegations at God.

We stand before God's idol and cry before Him or fight with Him. "Why are You making me suffer so much, God? What is my mistake? What have I done to go through this pain? Why don't You get me out of these difficulties? Are You there, God, or am I worshipping a stone idol? And if You are there, then why don't You answer my prayers? Why me, God, why me??"

If one is to think rationally, one would come to realize that God has no hand in all these situations. Don't we know fully well that our lives are a sum total of our own good and bad actions... our karmas? 'As you sow, so shall you reap' is a universally accepted truth and all religions come together in this belief. Our present and future are nothing but a reflection of our past deeds. One good deed comes back tenfold and one evil deed comes back hundredfold. Then why blame God?

When Baba was alive, He once got very annoyed with a particular devotee. This devotee had lost his only son due to a fatal disease. He loved Baba very much and cried inconsolably before His picture and in all his anguish kept repeating, "Baba, why did You take my son away? Why did You leave me and my wife to suffer? What is our mistake? Why did You snatch our only child away?" ... and so on. Later, when he visiled Bataa at Shirdi, Baba got wild when He saw him. He drove him out of the Dwarkamai and would not allow him to climb its steps and re-enter.

Then, after some time, Baba calmed down and permitted the devotee to entei. He then said affectionately, "You blame Me for all your sufferings. Do ! kill people's children or snatch them away? You pay for your own deeds. I do nothing and 1 am only a witness to your actions."

Saying so, Baba's soft heart melted and He blessed the devotee," But I will do something, i will bring the same child back in your wife's womb."

True to Baba's word, the couple was blessed with a son within a year. ☺

Delving deeper into this incident, one would realize once again that whatever we undergo in our life is a result of our own karmas and is not any kind of punishment thrust upon us by God. On the contrary, if we think and analyse this truth profoundly, we come across a very beautiful explanation for our endless sufferings. **One big sorrow takes us a hundred steps towards God, whereas one big happiness takes us a hundred steps away from God.** When in sorrow, we are drawn towards God as He is the only source of faith and hope in our lives. But when in happiness, we drift away from the Almighty, as we are lost in the pleasures and joys that come our way.

Our scriptures stand witness to the truth that the Lord takes away all material possessions only from those whom He especially loves. The idea is not lo punish or bring sufferings to them. On the contrary, by His special grace, man starts dwelling upon the meaning and purpose of life and acquires virtues and wisdom. He comes closer to the Lord as never before. Sorrows, sufferings and misfortunes along life's path should not make a man cynical, bitter or self-sympathetic. **In fact, problems are opportunities to look within and evolve. Each fall should become a reason to rise, and each hurdle a reason to move on.**

God's love for His children can be compared to a mother's love for her child: it is self-sacrificing and selfless. As says the Sai Satcharita, "A mother cleans and bathes her child, despite his wails and cries and even forces down bitter medicine to keep the child in good health and cleanse him of all diseases." Similarly, when our life is in turmoil, it means that He is cleansing and purifying us. Just as gold has to pass through a furnace before it glows brighter, we are made to undergo pain and suffering so that we come out cleansed of our negatives and our sins and emerge stronger, with hearts that are illumined by His divine presence.

If man were to sit and analyse each misfortune with a peaceful mind, he would realize that each suffering was actually a gift from God. When in sorrow we may not be able to see with clarity the positive force behind all negativity. But on contemplating in retrospect, we realize that it is indeed true that every cloud has a silver lining, and every windfall a lesson to teach. If we hold on steadfast, with our faith firm in God, each loss would make us stronger and each misfortune would energize us. Pain creates a special bonding between God and His children, which no happiness, however big, can. So thank God for every sorrow and let each loss make you a person of wisdom and immense inner strength.

As I move on, I'd like to share with all of you one of my most beautiful experiences of faith and perseverance; of how I bonded with Baba and submerged into the mould of His love; of how sorrows made us, Guru and disciple, One Inseparable Soul.

Nothing, absolutely nothing misses ihe all-pervading eyes of our dearest liaha. **Sometimes, a single, pure-hearted prayer is**

enough and sometimes it takes years of patience and undiluted, unswerving faith but finally He does respond. There can be no disputes, no arguments about why His response is instant at times and at other times it is delayed. This is because He alone knows what is best for us and also what is the best time to grant us our wishes and prayers. Therefore, we should have no doubts whatsoever and just trust Him completely. His decision has to be the best decision for us... His time to answer our prayers has to be the best time to answer our prayers. No one and nothing can be above our Raba Sai... so just have faith and don't count the hours, days or months. Leave everything up to His Divine Will and to His discretion. Trust Him completely; never stop praying or seeking His blessings. As far as the wishes of our heart are concerned, who, just who would know them better or clearer than our Baba. No words need to be spoken in prayer as He resides in our heart — our heart where each prayer has its origin. So He hears the prayers silently within, even before they can reach our mind or our lips. And He alone knows how and when to grant what we pray for. So just have faith, be patient and leave the rest unto Him.

On 12 June, 2003, I, along with a group of Baba's devotees, organized a Sai btiajan in the house of a very pious Kashmir! family: you know them by now. I am referring to the Raina family of Kashmir. A breathtaking durbar of Baba's pictures had been set up, and in the midst of tamps, lights and candles, His face shone with extraordinary grace and beauty. It felt as though the doors to heaven had been opened to us and we could walk right in and embrace our love... our Baba.

At this time, 1 was going through one of the most difficult phases of my life. Kumar, my (then) to-be husband was suffering unbearable agony and trauma. The last few years had been very tough for him. He had lost a lot of money in his business due to some fraudulent actions of his partners and was under a debt of millions of rupees. But like all other children of Baba, he too had not given up. Kumar had and still has tremendous fighting spirit. So he put all his savings and funds together, took some loans from banks, and with a lot of courage purchased a plot of land, which, by Baba's grace, he was getting at a very reasonable price. He decided to buy it and either start some business there or sell it off at a higher price in order to get rid of his debts. It took a lot of effort to get all the money together, as it was a huge amount and he was already in severe debt. But then, by the grace of Baba, he did manage to make the complete payment and on 2 December, 2002, he finally bought the plot of land.

We were all very relieved and as a sign of my deep gratitude towards Baba, 1 visited His temple each morning, at 4,30am, for His snan (bath) and Kakaei Aarti for 11 consecutive days (from. 11-22 Dec.}. I still remember, very clearly, that it was during those blissful days that I Started hearing Baba's voice in my heart and then soon we were having a lot of father-daughter conversations. ☺ This is when I bonded with Baba, like never before.

Then, in the midst of these few days of happiness, on 6, February, 2003, the biggest bad news of our life broke hell on us. A land mafia (goon) had forcefully taken possession of our plot, had also manipulated people and papers within the governing body and got a cancellation notice Issued to us. We had no due as to what was happening. We were simple people and, to be honest, we didn't even know who land mafias were. The only place where we had heard about such goons was in movies or in newspapers. On further enquiry, we came to know that this man was one of the most powerful people in the state, with assets worth billions. He followed this modus operand! in most of the cases and had thus amassed a lot of wealth. Ordinary people like us and several others neither had the backing nor the money to fight against such a powerful thug. We were shattered. Kumar was already neck deep in debts and now his only possession that could have saved him from going deeper and under, so to speak, had been mercilessly snatched away from him.

But Baba's children are brave children. They don't give up easily, as Baba blesses them with oodles and oodles of courage and also the conviction to face, fight and emerge victorious

against all odds. So we didn't give up, either. Kumar rushed to the local court. Nothing fruitful happened, so he went to the high court in a far-away city. Finally, on 28 February, 2003, he managed to get a stay order from the court against the cancellation notice. This was a temporary relief though, as a larger battle was yet to be waged.

More than three months had gone by. The situation had gone from bad to worse. The mafia had used his wealth tn its full potential. So, we were losing in court and the millions of rupees paid by us to the authorities, for the land, too stood forfeited. And what happened next was absolutely unbelievable.

One evening, when Kumar stepped out of his office, the goon's criminal recruits were waiting next to his car. Camouflaged by the twilight, they put a gun to his head. "Back out from the case, else we'll shoot you dead. Today, we have come to warn you. But next time, it will be your end."

This was our plight. Any normal person would shrivel in fear in such a trying situation. Loss of money can be handled but not at the cost of loss of life. ☺

1 loved Kumar too much to ever imagine a life without him. The thought of losing him was the last thought that 1 ever wanted to cross my mind. I knew in my heart that for the mafia to have him shot was a very minor thing. 1 saw Kumar in trauma: he had no money, no help or support and nothing good coming his way either. But I was his support because my Father Sai was my support. So despite the surmounting tensions, I had no fears. Honestly, I was never scared... not of the mafia, not of his men, not of their guns and not of his looting away our land. Baba's Udi was our armour against every peril. Each time Kumar left the house, we applied Udi to his forehead. And a forehead that bears the Udi cannot be pierced by bullets.

I smile today, when I look back at those painful times and am in awe of Baba's love. As unbelievable as it may be, the fact remains that nothing could shake me up or worry me. I don't deny being in pain because life's biggest trial is to see people you love suffering. But then, I also knew Baba was our unbreakable, impenetrable shield. No evil aiuld touch us as long as Baba was with us and this faith kept me lirlniniing with strength even at the most trying moments. The days were lough but our faith was tougher.

Coming back to where I began this story— 12th June, the evening of the bhajari at the Raina residence. My troubles had by now reached their peak. My heart was pining for Kumar's welfare and happiness. And i won't deny, I was losing courage, seeing him suffer so much. In tears, I bowed before Baba's durbar. As usual, Kumar was, at this moment, in a train bound for the high court. This had become a routine affair in our lives. He was travelling almost every alternate day. There was a hearing in the court and situations were totally in control of the mafia. We had come to know through our contacts thai large amounts of money had exchanged hands and the ruling in court was most likely to go against us. As 1 sat before the brightly burning lamps and looked at Baba in desolation, a sudden thought crossed my mind. I felt a rush of blood through my entire being. In a moment, my helplessness had changed hands with deep, inner strength and I was vibrant with courage once again. It was as though Baba had shown me a new path.

I had been feeling very low because there was absolutely no contribution that I had made or could make towards Kumar's problems, barring moral support and my prayers. I wanted to do much more. And now, by Baba's grace, I knew exactly what that was.

A beautiful incident narrated in the Sai Satcliarita had flashed through my mind and lit up a lamp in my heart. It was about a merchant, whose servant had whipped off all his life's savings, while he lay asleep.

As he sat moaning, a passing fakir (who was none other than Baba Himself) stopped by and spoke to him, "There is, in a place called

Shirdi, a merciful saint called Sai Baba. Bow mentally before Him and promise to give up your favourite food till you get back your lost wealth and take His darshan,"

The merchant, with complete faith, prayed to Baba and gave up rice, which he loved eating. He mentally promised Baba that he would now eat rice only at Baba's feet, after getting back his lost wealth. Baba's grace shone upon him and in a short span of 15 days, the Brahmin servant came back of his own accord, returned the stolen money and wept to be pardoned and spared the crime. How beautiful is the grace of our Baba Sail! He changed the thoughts of the Brahmin, made him realize his mistake and sent him back to the merchant. The grateful merchant then visited Baba at Shirdi, thanked Him and started eating rice once again. ☺

This little story became my inner strength, my courage. I decided then and there that 1 would now on transform all my negative energy into positive energy and fortitude. It was an overwhelming feeling; a feeling of discovering a spring in the desert, that too when death due to thirst, seemed inevitable. I was within these few magical moments very confident that Kumar would be victorious despite all odds.

1 immediately bowed before Baba's enthralling durbar and spoke to Him, "Baba, You know how I love eating rice; can't imagine a single day without it. So with all my faith, I too, like the merchant am giving up my favourite food... rice. Baba, Your son is in unbearable pain. I don't even know how long he will be able to go on like this. His life is in danger and his health is going from bad to worse. Kumar has even started showing suicidal tendencies. He prefers to end his life, rather than go through this pain. You have to save us, Baba. You are our Father and we know no one else other than You. Please, Baba, come to our rescue. And today before You, I promise, Baba, that I am giving up eating rice till the time Kumar is completely free of his problems and till he has paid off the last penny of his debts. We don't want to hold any such money that does not belong to us. We are not wrong in our intentions, Baba, just unfortunate. I will now eat rice

only when he rightfully gets back his land, utilizes it to pay back his huge debt and only when not a single penny is outstanding against him. And yes, Baba, whenever this sankalp (resolution) is completed, I will come to Shlrdi and eat rice from Your hands only."

I felt relieved and started awaiting a miracle just like the mefthant and thought in my heart that maybe in a time span of 15 days, Kumartoo would be able to pay back his debts and get back his land. But this was not to be. There were problems, problems and problems galore. The threats on gunpoint, the legal hassles, the ignominy before those whose money had to be repaid, all went on interminably. The situation further deteriorated but there was a certain pattern in the occurrence of events. The pattern was that things would go totally out of control and then there would suddenly be hope. Situations were against us, but after every dark tunnel we would see a gush of light, a ray of hope. The end result of this negative-positive combination was that we never lost the strength of our mind. Every time the black jaws of destiny tried to strangle us to death, Baba's benevolent hand came to save us and lend us support.

There is a heart-warming description of the Guru's love in the Satcliarita, in which Baba gives a divine narrative, of how He met His own Guru. Baba says, brimming with love, "By merely looking at My Guru, I would forget every thought of hunger or thirst. The world around would cease to exist, just divine eternal bliss would remain." When Baba's Guru appeared before Him for the very first time, He said to Baba, "You can come along with Me and 1 will lead the way. But only he who trusts in Me and has complete faith in Me shall be benefited." Baba decided to go along and follow Him with complete surrender. His Guru immediately took Him to a well and tethered His feet to the high branch of a tree close by, thereby suspending Him with a rope, head down and feet on top, hanging in mid-air, slightly above the water in that well. He left Baba there and went away for quite a few hours. On coming back, he quickly released Baba from that position of extreme discomfort and asked, "How are you? How did you fare?" And Baba flashed back a huge smile, "In Bliss Supreme

I was."

There is a deep lesson — an interpretation — interwoven in this conversation of Baba with His Guru. With the grace of Baba, what I derive from the narrative is that the Guru knows what is best for us. So, we must trust Him without doubt or question. The first thing Baba's Guru did on meeting Him, was to suspend Him in the most challenging, testing position. My understanding says that, when our Guru comes into our lives, He puts us through a test for the firmness of our faith. We have to prove worthy of being accepted by Him. And our faith and our worth are tested by the toughest of trials, by the most turbulent of storms. Baba shakes up our very existence 'upside down' (please note the symbolism in Baba's example of being suspended feet up and head down). Those that can't withstand the tests, walk away from their Guru, wither out and fall off like vulnerable leaves that can't withstand the raging winds. But those that hold on with utmost faith and unquestioned surrender, and smile through the troubled times with undiminishing confidence in their Guru, attain His love and support to eternity.

We had also met our dear Baba very recently. And I guess, we were also being tested, whether we weie worthy of His love or not. The test was tougher than I had ever imagined bul, then, we were Baba's children and clung un to His garb with faith, even though suspended in mid-air.

Time went by and my 15 days of giving up rice turned into weeks, then months and then years. The debts kept increasing and our willpower kept decreasing. The only one thing that didn't change was our faith in Baba. On the other hand, Kumar and my wedding could not materialize as he did not want to risk my life along with his own. The struggle went on and side-by-side stories of little victories and large blessings of Baba kept getting created.

I had started readings of the Sai Satcharita and continued doing Saptali after Saptah, week by week, month after month. 1 also did several Chalisa readings and my faith only grew stronger with each passing day. This faith I infused into Kumar, who was already abundant with his own faith in Baba. His courage and conviction were gifts from Baba and lie made the best out of them. My parents, my sister, Kumar's side of the family, our dear friends... all were praying along. And yes, from whatever little money we could save, which wasn't much, we did a lot of charity day by day. I would literacy pull Kumar along, through his troubles and we would feed slum children, visit old-age homes, orphanages, children of criminals who had been jailed and so on. I knew from personal experience (of my birth) that charity is such a beautiful act that it neutralizes the impact of all past negative karmas and bestows joy. So, we did loads of that too. Our belief remained firm; a belief that Baba's love sustains us even when there is no other nourishment available. Anyone and everyone may forsake us but Baba would never forsake us.

Time passed on mercilessly and our prayers went on unabated. Four years of the struggle had gone by. Kumai also joined me in doing endless, uncountable Saptah.i of Baba's SaTchurita. We would begin together and end together, week after week. I think that is what Baba was waiting for. He wanted undiluted faith, dedicated love and ardent devotion from Kurnai. He had always loved Baba but now I saw a different person in him. Earlier, my faith used to nurture his faith. But today, he had developed his own special bond of love with Baba; today he had faith that Baba would bring him out of this hell. My lonesome prayers were probably not enough. ☺

I also managed to compel Kumar to place his fears of threat to my safety and my life at Baba's feet, marry me and accept me in his life. I believed deep within that my stars when fused with that of Kumar's, in marital bliss, would bring him loads of good luck. So, finally after a long wait of several years, Kumar accepted me in his life. © We got married at Shirdi, on 30 September, 2006, in a small ceremony, in the presence of Baba and our family. In fact, we look the seven customary pheras around Baba's picture and got bonded together for births to come with Baba's grace.

Two months had gone by. We were carrying out yet another reading of the Satcharita when the final hearing of the case came up. I had accompanied Kumar to the city where the hearing was to be held in the High Court.

On the morning of the hearing, an unknown, elderly gentleman walked up to Kumar in the court room and placed in his hands some prasad. When Kumar looked up in surprise, he smiled, "All will be well." Saying this, he went in and sat down on the window sill of the court room.

At the same time, when Kumar was in court, I decided to visit Baba's temple and distribute food amongst poor children. There, outside the temple, I saw an elderly man. He was shivering due to cold: it was 23rd December and there was severe chill in the air. I walked up to him and said, "Baba, come along with me. I'll buy you something warm."

He happily tagged along. There were shops near the temple from where 1 got him a pullover. He appeared so happy... 1 can't describe it in words. He kept his hand on my head and smiled, "All will be well." (Gosh! 1 am crying as 1 write this.)

Just then, my phone rang. It was Kumar! I said a short prayer and received the call. After years I heard that voice, "Puja, we have won the case!" He was screaming in delight. ☺

1 wanted to dance in the middle of the street. 1 turned around in ecstasy to hand over some money to the old Baba, so that he could buy some sweets too and celebrate our joy. But he had vanished right before my eyes. And in the court room, Kumar ran to the window to thank the old man, dressed in white. But the window was empty. ☺ He came. He blessed, He disappeared.

Winning the case was the first step. The paperwork that had changed hands with money in the authority office had to be turned around and a lot of officials who had sold their morals to the mafia had Lo be taken care of. We were still praying. Kumar and I continued the Satcharita reading. My Papa was praying, my Maa was doing a path, my sister was chanting, all other family members and friends were pleading before Baba, while Kumar and I were living, breathing and iriVoking Sai at every moment. And then the inevitable happened. *"

Kumar received a call from someone. We didn't know him, nor did we know how he reached us. He lived in a temple of Baba, several hundred kilometres from where we lived.

On that call, this elderly man's first words were, "Aum Sai Shri Sai Jaya Jaya Sai."

Wondering who he was, Kumar repeated, "Aum Sai Shri Sai }aya Jaya Sai."

He then kept chanting different mantras of Baba and made Kumar chant all of them, after him. He then said, "1 know how much you have suffered. Baba has sent me to help you."

Kumar went to meet him and was handed over documentary evidence against the mafia and also the officials — the government servants — who were working underhand for the mafia. And once Kumar brought this evidence into limelight, a series of miracles began. The media got all diarged-up and the mafia's misdeeds unfolded before the world. Kumar was on TV and in the newspapers. People who read his story were horrified and several came out to help him. Til! now we were struggling all alone and here we were surrounded by a thousand hands of mir Baba Sai. The wrongdoers in the authority office were pulverized by the media. And finally, the big day dawned... the mafia was arrested and Kumar was handed back the legal papers of his land. ☺

Baba had woven us into His miracle. We were flying high. Kumar got his land back and he immediately sold it out for fear of further trouble. He received the first major payment against it, which was sufficient to pay off all his debts. And guess what?? Baba dear had shown His acceptance of my devotion; as the day he received the money, was the same day on which I had given up eating rice. Yes, four years later, on the same day — 12 June, 2007 — Kumar's miseries came to an end. ☺

During these difficult years, there were, at all times, hundreds of people against us but one Baba alone, standing by us, standing by our truth, was infinitely more powerful than the hundreds against us. ☺

What are we... nothing more than greedy, thankless creatures? All we know is to ask, beg and plead and when our wish is fulfilled, after a few grateful words, we move on. And what is He?? He is our benevolent, gracious Father who never ever forsakes His children. He is our life-force. He is our reason to live. He is every breath we take. We are nothing without Him. So every day must begin and end with a pure prayer of gratitude... gratitude for the little and big mercies that He bestows upon us every day, every moment. Don't ask, because by asking you limit His blessings. If you ask, you get only what you ask for, hut if you only pray for His never-ending grace in your life, you end up getting far more. Does He not know our heartfelt wishes?? He resides in our heart and He knows best what we wish for. So just pray for His blessings and be grateful for them. Trust Him completely and unquestioningly. Kumar and I only prayed for inner strength and His blessings... and He gave us far beyond our expectations. These four years of suffering gave us a new life. We were reborn as Baba's true children and now our life, our breath, our heartbeat are all dedicated to His service.

Slowly, steadily everything got back to normal. Kumar settled all his debts. Now the time had finally come for me to start eating rice. I had really yearned to eat it all these years and here I was so close to tasting rice cmce again.

Baba called us to Snirdi and soon the entire family was off to thank dearest Baba. We — Kumar, 1 and our entire family — left for Shirdi on 11 October, 2007. The first delightful darshan of Baba at His

Samadhi Mandir was all purifying and blissful. We wept, we flooded Uaba's temple with tears of gratitude. We were blessed with a divine feeling, of bring relieved from overloads of burden, as we realized that the worst was dually over. ☺ And, of course, I was also smiling through my tears, due in the excitement of getting to eat rice, after so many long years.

After Baba's preliminary darshan, we went to a restaurant, in order to eat something. My little sister, Neha, was really happy for me and deeply wished to see me eat rice in my very first meal at Shirdi. But she was in for complete disappointment as 1 refused to do so. I had my emotional reasons for this. I was to eat rice after a very patient wait of four years and four months anil a very long struggle. I had made up my mind years ago that the first grain of rice that I would eat had to come from my dearest Baba's hands. Everyone in my family got really upset with me for this decision.

Neha spoke up, annoyed, while Kumar smiled, "Hasn't Baba done enough for you already? You are now in Shirdi as per your wish, you've thanked Baba and taken His darshan; now why the delay? You know very well that Baba has taken Stimadhi. Then how do you expect Him to come and feed you rice?"

But 1 was adamant because 1 had promised Baba years back that whenever He would take us out of our large, looming trouble, He would also have to feed me with the first grains of rice.

So 1 replied, "Please don't be upset with me, I know very well that Baba has already given us far 7~nore than our expectations or wants. But at the same time, try to understand my sentiments. I am not asking Baba to come down in His human form. I just want that someone here in Shirdi, in any mop, any form, should give me rice to eat. And I'll accept it as Baba's blessing and as His prasad. But 1 will not eat rice myself... even if that translates to going hack from Shirdi without eating rice."

My family gave in to my emotions and kept silent over the matter, though 1 could see Neha was still visibly upset, thanks to her deep love and concern for me.

It was time for the noon aarti and so we finished our meal and rushed to Baba's Dwarkamai. Baba's aarti is always enthralling and mesmerizing. We sang along, clapped in joy and celebrated His name. We were just walking out after the aarti when the elderly panditji came out with a big bowl and beckoned to us and also to the other devotees standing around us to come forward and take Baba's prasad. In the Dwarkamai, we get Ghana Prasad (black grams and sugar-coated sweet). 1 walked up and stretched out my hand to receive the same; and into my hand poured Baba's divine grace, His benevolence, and His love. Yes, in ray palm was a handful of rice! Tears flowed down my eyes. Years of wait and my penance had finally ended and I could not have asked for more. There could be no better person to hand out the first grains of rice, than Baba's elderly punditji. And there certainly could be no better place than Baba's home, His Dwarkamai.

As I stood numb with disbelief and looked on at the Rice Prasad in my palm, Neha rushed towards me with a big smile, raised my palm up using her own palm and pushed the rice into my mouth and screamed ecstatically, "Di, finally an end to your Rice Sacrifice." ©

We learnt the meaning of Faith, we got the lesson of Patience, we imbibed the Strength of the Satcharita; we realized the Power of the Udi and finally we bathed in the Grace of dear Baba. His love re-writes destiny, wipes out the darkness from our lives, illumines our world and bestows upon us the Armour of His Love. He intoxicates us with the charm of His Divine Eyes and then we live the rest on our lives enchanted, enamoured, inebriated by the Ambrosia called Sai. ☺ Love You, Baba. Love You Soooo Much.

Aum Stti Shri Sai faya faya Sai

"Mother, you have fed Me sumptuously up to my throat, My afflicted pranas (life-forces) have been satisfied. Always act like this., and this will stand you in good, stead. Sitting in this Masjid I shall never, never speak untruth. Take pity on Me like this. First give bread to the hungry, and then eat yourself. Note this well. Eating that lovely bread I am heartily contended and I am still belching. The dog, which you saw before meals and to which you gave the piece of bread is one- with Me, so also other creatures (cats, pigs, flies, cows, etc.) are one with Me. I am roaming in their forms. He who sees Me in all these creatures is My beloved. So abandon the sense of duality and distinction and serve Me as you did today."

— SAI BABA OF SHIRDI

You are my Moon, Baba

As a devotee is resolute and determined, so is Baba's immediate response. Sometimes Baba puts the devotees to severe test; and then gives them 'upadesh' (instructions).

Lord Krishna had appeared before Arjuna in His viraat mop (universal form), in which the entire universe, all the galaxies and milky ways and life in every form — from the largest creation to the tiniest — all appeared as existing within His Divine Form. The truth that Lord Krishna gave out to Arjuna continues to hold good even today. Baba, who to His children is no less than God Himself, is also one with nature. He is the stars, the mountains, the rivers, the oceans, the earth, the sky... He is the entire universe. Everything exists within Him and He exists in everything. And He has His special ways of showing us His oneness with nature; ways that cannot be described by words or limited by language... ways that only the heart can feel and discern.

Baba always taught the lesson of Cosmic Oneness. He said that the same soul that dwells within Him also dwells in animals, plants and all of nature. Once, a devotee, Mrs Tarkhad, fed a dog a slice of bread at noon, before going to the Dwarkamai to feed dear Baba. When she later reached the Dwarkamai with her offering of food, Baba said to her lovingly, "I need no more food, as by appeasing the dog's hunger you have already fed Me to My heart's content."

On another occasion, Baba told Lakshmi Bal Shinde, one of Baba's dearest and most intimate devotees, that He was very hungry and that she should get Him something to eat. She loved Baba dearly and could not bear the thought of Baba's hunger. So she rushed home in haste, cooked meals for Baba and ran back to the rnasjid to serve Baba her dish. Baba picked up the entire food cooked by her and fed it to a dog outside the tnasjid. Lakshmi Bai initially got very upset at Baba's action.

But then Baba spoke to her affectionately, "Why do you get upset for no reason? **Satiating the dog's hunger is equivalent to satiating My hunger. The animals are no different from Me. He who thus feeds them, actually feeds Me and gives Me immense happiness. Just as we feel weak and uneasy if we don't get the nourishment of food, so also all plants and animals feel hungry too. Always remember, he who feeds the hungry, appeases My Soul."**

What a delightful lesson was thus shared by Baba... a lesson of Cosmic Oneness of the Supreme Soul. We must always keep this lesson close to our heart and make sure that no creature goes on an empty stomach in our presence. **If each of us realizes our moral responsibility, no soul will go hungry on Mother Earth... because then there will always be more hands that feed than those that ask.**

1 had a divine experience of this Cosmic Oneness of Baba... in the most overwhelming, unearthly manner ever. It was on Saturday, 19 October, 2002. Some of our relatives had come over to our house. After lunch, as we sat down to chit-chat, the topic of discussion somehow shifted from that of routine conversations to spiritual matters. My elderly aunt insisted that God exists in all beings and also in nature in the subtle nirgun mop (formless state), which is not visible to our eyes; hut if anyone with a pure heart and with undying faith looks through the eyes of the heart, one would most certainly see God in every creation, even in the sagun wop (with body or form). 1 was really intrigued by her argument but found it hard to believe how one could see the sa%un form of God in nature.

She said rather arrogantly, "You children, today's generation, where do you have such deep faith, to witness such an extraordinary sight?"

This really disturbed me. A question had been raised on the depth of my faith and the faith of the so-called newer generation. This was just not fair. 1 was not ready to accept the statement hands down.

This incident took place in the same year, in which I had met Baba, known Baba. I win new In Baba and this new-found faith. And in a few months ol having found the love ot my life, the same love had been questioned, liven though the guests left our house, the thought would just not leave me. 1 had to go to a friend's wedding, along with my family that evening, but even there 1 was not in peace.

We reached home, well past midnight. 1 did not feel like sleeping because my thoughts were still causing a storm in my mind. So I walked out to the terrace of our apartment. The dark night was lit up by a bright full moon,

I looked up at the moon and the stars, and a thought flashed through my mind. Still looking up 1 spoke aloud, "Baba, I am really disturbed today. My aunt says that faithful, love-full devotees have seen the.ii isht (beloved deity) in different forms of nature, if they have called out with a pure heart. My love for You is pure too. Then why must 1 not get Your dnrshfln? It feels as though my faith is being tested. So, I am calling out to You, with all my love, Baba. 1 want to see You in Your sa$un form, in the moon. And Baba, if You don't appear, that according lo my aunt would imply that my love for You and my faith in You is lacking. And that just can't be. Come for me, Baba, come for my faith."

Saying this 1 started counting from ten backwards, and warned Baba, "Baba, 1 am counting from ten to one. And before I count 1, You must appear." Though on paper, this may sound like a threat of love but, in reality, 1 was so shaken up that day, so desirous of proving my love strong that 1 was in deep unease. My heart was palpitating faster than the speed of sound. Baba had to come.

10, 9, 8, 7, 6, 5... I was counting aloud, my heartbeat thundering within... 4, 3... Baba, please... 2... and ☺... behold... the moon was suddenly gelling brighter... so bright, that it was hurting my eyes. As 1 looked on in awe, forgetting to count my last number... the moon became brighter still... and my heart stopped thundering, maybe even beating... as before my eyes was my life's most beautiful visual.... The moon had become Baba!

Baba's glowing face smiled back at me. The moon had assumed the form of Baba's ever-smiling face. 1 was jolted inside out. ! wept and wept, scared that my tears should not wash away this breathtaking sight. But He stayed and smiled, while I trembled and cried. Ufffff!! I wish I could show you what I saw. I wish I could take you through the emotion 1 felt... ☺

Just then my mother, fuming, walked out onto the terrace, "It is 2am. Is this the time, for a girl to be standing outside? Come inside and sleep."

i think, she observed my gaze, because I didn't turn towards her, fearing that Baba may disappear.

Just then I heard a scream, "Oh Devaaoa\l It's Baba in the moon."

She screamed on ecstatically, before she broke down into tears. Yes, she had seen Him too. So, after all, I was not imagining it, I smiled. Maa's dramatic scream had broken my gaze but when 1 looked back, Baba was still there. 1 ran in, woke up Dad and my sis and they too witnessed the bliss of that Divine Night.

So, He came then and He comes even now but only on days (sorry, nights ☺), when my prayers are sincere, when I need Him most. He came that day to prove to me that my love was pure. How sweet is that?? We not only test Him to see whether He loves us deeply but also ask Him to answer, what our heart already knows... do we too love Him as deeply? It is like asking Him, "Do I love You, Baba?" ☺ As if my heart doesn't know the answer!! **What more proof do I need — do we need — that Baba is still alive?? He is glowing in the moon, twinkling in the stars, flowing in the rivers, shimmering in the sunshine, sparkling in the ocean, beating in our hearts, alive in every wee bit of this Universe and in our Souls.**

Aum Sal Shri Sai Jaya Jaya Sai

"If you spread your palms with devotion before Me, I am immediately with you, Any and night. Though, I am here bodily, still I know what you do, beyond the seven sects. Go wherever you mil, over the wide world, I nm with you. My abode is in your heart and I am within you. Always worship Me, Who is seated in your heart as well as in the hearts of all beings. Blessed and fortunate, indeed, is he who knows Me thus."

— SAI BABA OF SHIRDI

Baba, Please Say "I Love You" with a Red Rose

"Let My man (Devotee) be at any distance, a thousand kos away from Me, he will be drawn to Shirdi like a sparrow, with a thread tied to its feet."

A red rose, in the language of emotions, is an expression of love. Instead of saying the magical words "I love you", one can just give a red rose and the same sentiment would get conveyed. Similar has been the case in the beautiful relationship that I have shared with my love, my Baba. Each time I wished to say "1 Jove you", all I did was take a red rose to the temple and place it at His Holy Feet;

We were in Shirdi on our annual family visit. As always, we spent the most blissful days with Baba and now it was finally time to depart. Our cab had to leave Shirdi in the next half hour for Manmad, from where we had to board a train to Delhi. It was customary for me to seek Baba's blessings in the Samadhi Mandir, before starting back home. I always took His permission and said my final goodbye to Him before leaving. But this day was different.

It was raining in torrents, I got delayed and there was no time left for my final darshan of Baba. In half an hour, we had to leave and it was almost impossible to meet Baba because in the evenings the Samadhi Mandir would be crowded to suffocation and it would take no less than two hours for Baba's darahan. All the same, I was determined to meet Baba and bid Him goodbye. And to be honest, there was another big reason as well, 1 had presented a red rose at Babd's feet earlier that evening. I was brimming with love for my Baba and expressed my emotions for Him with the gift of the rose. But the flood of my emotions didn't stop thereafter as I deeply craved for Baba's response and that too in the same manner. Yes, 1 wanted Baba to give me a red rose, if He too loved me. © So despite the objections raised by my mother and the annoyance of my father — at the possibility of missing the train — I ran towards Baba's Samadhi Mandir, to bid Him goodbye; at the same time, rightfully expecting a rose from Him.

With crossed fingers and a sincere prayer on my lips for a miracle — because only a miracle could get me Baba's danlian within half an hour — 1 entered the huge hall where hundreds of devotees stood In a queue to get a glimpse of Baba.

1 walked in and looked around, "Have I entered the wrong hall? Where are the queues of devotees?"

The place was completely empty. I could not see a single devotee around and as I turned back to leave, still wondering if I had come into the wrong place, 1 heard a voice.

It was the security guard, "Why are you going back? Don't you wish to take Baha's darshari?"

"Yes, of course I do," 1 replied.

"Then go straight inside," he said.

"But where are the other devotees?" I asked.

He smiled, "It is strange, but today very few people have turned up for the diirshan. It is indeed a very rare sight to see these halls vacant. But that's the way it is. You are very fortunate. Just go straight in."

I could not believe that this was actually happening. I ran frantically, tears flowing down my eyes. Down the stairs, then up the stairs and here I was standing right before Baba's life-size idol. In precisely two minutes I had reached my Sai. I was still breathless when I suddenly noticed that though the halls outside — at the entry point — were empty, here inside it was packed to full capacity. There are, at all times, two queues in the Samadhi Mandir that move parallel to each other, towards Baba's Samadhi for darshan. There is one queue that moves towards Baba's head (as He lies in the Samadhi) and the other towards His feet. This evening was no different and devotees in both queues were lined-up, awaiting Baba's darshan.

There is an entry in the centre of the hall also, right in front of Baba where one could walk straight towards the Samadhi. But that was always kept closed and was only opened in rare cases for the diseased or crippled who could not stand in a queue. This entry was closed even today, as every other day, and huge ropes had been tied across to block the path.

Here I was, inside the Mandir, very close to Baba, but still so far. How do I reach Him? The queues inside the Samadhi Mandir were quite long and in no situation could I reach Baba in time.

In complete despair, 1 looked at Baba and prayed, "1 can't go without meeting You, Baba. And I will not go until 1 receive a red rose at Your feet. So please help me. Please, Baba, Please."

As 1 was praying, 1 observed a police inspector sitting in a corner and monitoring all the activities of the temple. An idea, obviously sent by my Baba Sai, flashed through my mind.

I closed my eyes, gathered my guts and walked towards him. "Sir, I need your help. I have to board a train and I'm very late. Can you please help me so that I can say goodbye to Baba before leaving? If [stand in the queue, I'll surely miss my train."

He looked at me, blank, expressionless and did not respond. I could feel tears pricking my eyes as 1 waited. And I think the inspector saw them too, for he suddenly stood up and signalled towards me to follow him.

Behold the grace of dear Baba! The unbelievable was happening again.

He walked right to the centre of the Mandir, lifted up the strong ropes tied across to block the entry and signalled once again with his hand for me to walk straight towards Baba's huge idol. I could not believe this was actually happening. Precisely five minutes back, 1 had no clue whether I would be able to meet Baba or not. And here I was standing all alone, no queues around me, getting a 'royal goodbye darshan' from Baba. © The same security people, who normally move us out in haste — to make place for more devotees — were giving me a VIP treatment.

I walked straight ahead towards Baba's Samadhi and His breathtakingly beautiful idol. 1 still had 25 minutes to spare. And no one was asking me to leave, not even the security. So I sat down right in front of Baba and wept endlessly. The tears 1 shed were tears of love, tears of gratitude and tears of separation... flowing all together, at the same time. I always detest the moments when I have to leave Shirdi. It feels as if someone is ripping me apart and separating me from my Father. But then, one has to go. So after looking at His Divine Form and absorbing it within every bit of my being, 1 stood up to leave. 1 walked towards Baba's Samadhi, bowed down with reverence and stood.... Well, I had still not received my goodbye rose. I kept standing and hoping that Baba would send a signal to the panditji, to give a rose to His daughter. But no, it was not to happen. How long could 1 stand there, after all? And I was determined not to ask for one. If Baba loved me, then He Himself should give me a rose. Did I not of my own wish get roses for Him now and then as an expression of my love? But despite the long wait, I got no rose and now 1 started feeling very bad. It almost felt as if Baba was annoyed with me for some reason and did not wish to even express His love for me. So, I started walking back, teais flowing down even more profusely than before.

As l was walking back towards the rope from where 1 had got in, I observed someone gesturing towards me. A devotee standing in the queue (towards Baba's head) was calling me. 1 walked towards him. He gestured for me to get in the qutue and stand in front of him. The queue was moving towards Baba's idol and this elderly gentleman who had called out to me, was about to reach Baba's Samadhi. Still puzzled, my vision blurred due to my tears, I got into the queue. In another minute, I was standing next to Baba's Samadhi once again, this time towards His head.

Baba's devotees who have visited Shirdi can well imagine and visualize what was happening. Shirdi is almost always extremely crowded and devotees barely manage to get Baba's darshan before being ushered out of the Mandir by the security. And here 1 was, getting my life's most memorable darshan, first from the centre and now towards Baba's head.

Who was this old gentleman? Why did he call me? Did he feel sorry to see rtie shedding tears? But so many devotees shed tears of love when they stand before Baba's divine form! Had Baba sent him? Maybe Baba had called me back to give me the rose? So I again bowed before Baba anil waited patiently for the rose. But no luck this time, too. 1 genuinely can't express what I was feeling at that moment; the gratitude for such a divine darshan, the sorrow of parting from Baba and the pain of not getting the rose. So, once again after waiting and still not getting the rose, I decided to leave. I bid Baba my final goodbye and left the Mandir with a heavy heart. I didn't want to leave but now time had run out and 1 was getting late for my train. So 1 got no rose, bid farewell to Baba arid walked out through the door, still miserably tearful.

And... and it happened yet again. Two people standing right outside that door signalled to me. Now who were they? One of them was wearing a uniform and had a broom in his hand. He appeared to be a sweeper attendant of Baba's Mandir and the other man was clad in the ethnic clothes and turban that Baba's official attendants (bhaldan) wear. I did not understand the language they spoke. So, for the third time this evening, sign language was used. They opened up the knots of yet another rope and signalled for me to walk through. Still confused, 1 followed one of them. And no one can imagine where he rook me!

He made me enter Baba's Samadhi Mandir once again, this time from the back door, at Ihe exit point. And unbelievable as it may sound, here I was standing next to Baba's Samadhi, but this third time, 1 was towards His feet, I really didn't know what was happening with me. Who were all these people? Why were they going out of the way and helping me? What was my dearest Baba doing? In my entire life, 1 had never ever got such a majestic and enthralling darshan; first from the front, then towards the side of Baba's head in His Samadhi and now finally towards His feet. And I was sure, this was also the last time I was getting such a tianhan because heaven does not make us human beings tread its path again and again so easily. So, I bowed at Baba's silver feet that are placed next to the Samadhi and my tears bathed them with love and giatitude. I can't find the right words to give expression, to what 1 felt during those divine moments. But I'm sure Baba's devout hhaktas can feel my emotions, experience my sentiments when they visualize all that I was blessed with that evening.

I looked at Baba with my blurred vision for the final time, said goodbye and with happy memories turned to leave. A lady in security uniform stopped me at the door and signalled towards Baba's idol. God! Sign language once again. Now what? 1 turned and walked back and looked towards Baba's idol, still wondering. Panditji Looked at me, turned towards Baba's idol, picked up a bunch of three red roses lying at Baba's Holy Feet, turned again towards me and stretched out his hand... the hand that held the roses... for me, 1 heard a voice; a voice that came from my heart. 1 stretched my hands to receive the roses and that voice echoed within me and said, "1 love you, 1'uja." ☺

So kind is our father.... Let us just love Him madly. In fact, let us go insane in His love. Let our love be an obsession, a craze. Love Him in any way, in any relationship. But love Him. Love Him as your Father Sai Baba, as your Mother Sal Maa, as your brother or sister or friend. Or just fall in love with Him and let Him be your love, your Sai. Be in love with Him. Let no other sentiment be stronger, no other relation bigger than the one you share with your Sai, your liaba. Because the more you live Him, the more He loves you. The deeper you dive in His love, more precious the gems you get from the bottom of the ocean of love, called Baba. **Love Him so much that He can't stay**

without your love. Make Him so dependent on your love that He ties that never-ending bond with you for all your births to come.

And now visualize the end of such love, of such a bonding; an end that is a beginning, the first step towards merging in Him. Open the eyes of your heart and envision.... **You are running towards Him, madly in love with Him, towards His abode, up above in the heavens. You can't wait to get to Him and merge in Him forever. You run up the long staircase, towards the deep blue sky. The climb is long and steep, but you don't tire because your love provides you the energy and the strength. And finally, as you walk through the puf fed-up, preening clouds and reach the last step, what do you see? You see your Sai, dressed in a white, flowing robe; divine, blissful, surrounded by a golden-white, resplendent aura... standing before you. You are breathless, you are crying, you are laughing, you are craving, you are celebrating the joy of having reached His feet. And as you look on, He tilts His head to one side affectionately and His divine eyes penetrate through you like lightning. He then smiles His most calming and charismatic smile and slowly His hand stretches out to welcome you. And in this heavenly white, spotless picture, you suddenly see colour... for the hand, Baba's hand, that stretches out towards you, speaks in silence, speaks with colour... the colour of love... the colour of luscious red rases. ☺ Yes, for all those years, those births that you have spent loving Him, He gives His final response, with bouquets of red roses in His outstretched hand and says with His warmest smile, "1 love you too, my child."**

Your eyes are blurred by a fountain of tears but you still run towards the bright visible colour and grab the roses in your hand. And then as you look at Him, your eyes meet, magic happens: the world melts below your feet, everything ceases to exist and then the wall that has separated you from Him, falls apart... and you merge in Him for ever... and ever. ☺

Aum Sai Shri Sai Jaya Jaya Sai

Epilogue

Thousands of years ago, Shri Krishna had stepped down to save the earth. And in the Kali Yuga, Baba came down as our saviour, our hope, our destiny. His fullness replenished, our hollow emptiness and gave a meaning to our directionless life. His love lit up a million stars to brighten our dark, lonely nights. Our fears took flight and what remained was passion and power, exuded by His Divine Love, Before Baba came into our world, we were drifting in flowing water purposelessly nut His Presence steered us on the right course and powered us towards our goals, our destination. Today, our lives have a deeper meaning and a higher purpose, all gratitude to Baba.

Of the many gifts that our merciful Sai has bestowed upon us... this book is one too. As mentioned earlier, Baba blessed me in my dream and He metamorphosed into this book that you hold in your hands today. This is not a material gift of printed paper but a spiritual gift of invaluable blessings. **Thus spoke the Lord God. our Guru Sai in His Guruvaani, "1 present to you Myself in the form of this transcendent abundance. The words of this book are mine, their priceless wealth yours. He who imbibes my teachings and lives a life of righteousness and detached action shall attain bliss in this world and that. Every time you need Me, you shall find Me next to yoti. My soul shall converse with you, through the ink on these pages. Your doubts shall be resolved, your queries remedied. Reading this book with faith shall alleviate your pain and suffering, bestow upon you everlasting bliss and happiness. And those that believe in Me, firm and heart-strong, shall be brought back from the doon of heaven and blessed with a life anew. These are My words... the words of your Sai, laden with unquestioned truth. Those that trust in Me, I shall carry them in My arms across the seven seas, through hot burning sands and over the toughest peaks. You will feel Me, holding you, next to My heart, wrapped in My strong arms.**

Those that are connected to Me, with innermost depths of their souls, shall feel My breath, hear My heartbeat and experience My presence in a million colourful ways. Whenever the clouds are fierce, the storm is raging tumultuously and your ground is shaky, hold Me... The Book... next to your bosom and the sky will shine a deep blue again. I shall draw you out from the most virulent challenges, but for that you must lay complete faith in My feet and keep the flame of patience ever ablaze. I give you My assurance, that anyone who resorts to these old, holy feet shall never he turned back empty handed. I was yours, 1 am yours and I shall remain yours. The whole world may forsake you, hut your Baba will always stand by you, as your guiding star and lead you on the Golden Path... the path on which, I am the traveller, I am the journey, 1 am the destination."

So, with the grace of my Big Daddy, my Baba Sai... I humbly hand over this book in your hands, in your care. 1 pray that this work by none other than our Lord Sai Himself, empowers your thoughts, refurbishes your faith and brightens your world. Believe in Baba, lay your life in His feet and He shall look after you like a Divine Mother. No harm will come to you if you surrender yourself with body, mind and soul before Him. Anyone who is in pain or who is finding it difficult to wage the battle of life, gift him/her this blessing of Sai. Soaking in the teachings of Baba, absorbing in the many lessons of true faith and devouring in the miraculous stories of belief and conviction, shall reaffirm the diminishing faith of many and re-instil in them the courage to move on.

If God were to step down and give in your possession a magic wand that could fulfil all your wishes without expecting anything in return, would you not treasure it, just as you treasure your life? So also, Baba has bequeathed this mesmerizing jewel in your hands... One Book that shall give you all you desire... name, fame, health, wealth, wisdom, success, virtues, values, peace, prosperity, joy, love, dreams, desires, bliss, salvation... and lots mine; because reading about Baba is as powerful and as blessed as being in 'His Living Presence'. And holding this book in the palms of your hands and guzzling it word by word, with a voracious, insatiable thirst... you will be reminded time and again that Baba has gone nowhere, that we are even today in His Living Presence... that Sai Baba Is Still Alive.

Aum Sai Ram!

Praise for the Book

Sai Baba Is Still Alive is a great book about my God; my Guru, my Soul - Shirdi Sai and His Leelas. It is one of the best books I have read in recent times. This book is very close to my heart and I am sure whoever reads it will feel the connect with Baba, which is mesmerizing. The lucid way in which, the author Ms. Jaya Wahi has expressed her deep love for Baba and her unique experiences, touch the reader's heart and inspire us to just love Him more and more.

- Vasanth. S. Sai
Film Director
National Award Winner
Kalaimamani

However you call madam, either JAVA WAHI or JAI SAIEE, it is ail the same. Though I am an ardent devotee of Sainath, somehow it took a long time to procure a copy of Sai Baba Is Still Alive for me. Oh My God after reading through pages after pages, my love with Sai has become multi-fold and strong. Tears roll down and drench me completely. I used to believe and sense Baba everywhere and every time but with knowledge gained from this book, I admit HE is still alive in one's heart as well.

Have no words for JAVA WAHI alias JAI SAIEE . She has articulated in such a way, that carry us and make us feel in the cosmic world and for sure Sainath has made her type / write. Please accept my sincere gratitud, namaskarams, salutations.

- Suresh Kumar OP
Verified Buyer
Amazon

The only book I have read that I can say actually truly changed my life... Each and every chapter gave me goose bumps and fresh lears which lent new depth to my belief & faith. This book Is my strength in every which way and fills me with hope & courage to face all of life's challenges on a daily basis clutch It close to my heart in moments of despair & HIP moment sure does pass!!! Thank u jaya... you are truly amazing and we are so blessed to have our paths cross.

- **Shalla Balerao**
Fashion Designer
Chennai

Baba Is Still Alive!!! What else can catch your attention more than that for Baba devotees? But, reading it was like living through every Leela mentioned in the book . After the Sai Satcharitra this book has changed my way of looking at life and has increased my faith in the belief that Baba is really with you every moment; yes, truly, every moment. For me, my Guru , who never ceases to amaze me so very often, takes me to new depths of devotion and deep thoughts of life and the hereafter. The more you read Sai Baba Is Still Alive, the more you become humble and bow down to him. Meeting Jaya Wahi in person makes you feel His presence, yes, this also is true!!

- **Imtiaz Pasha**
Business Owner
Chennai

Sai Baba Is Still Alive has been a ray of hope in the darkness of my life. I always loved Baba but faith and patience were taught to me by this book. I believe Baba came to me through this book. After reading it, I had such a strong desire to meet Di and that too happened miraculously. This book is a proof of Baba's love for us. It gives strength to the weak, solace to the meek, consolation to the troubled. Every experience written only reinstates His existence. By Baba's grace I always give a copy of this book to family and friends who seem troubled and they give me loads of blessings in return because this book does what it does best......create faith and hope. We can never thank Di enough for this book. It has not only touched many souls but it has transformed them. Aum Sai.

-Dimple Thakker
Senior Consultant
Audit & Assurance
Mumbai

For me this is not only a book about Sai Baba or about Jaya Maa. For me this is a door given to me by my lord to open and enter the world I always longed for. It introduced me to the Baba whom I knew, but was not sure where or how to find Him. He resolved that and gave me my Guru Jaya Maa. For me there is no difference between my Baba and my Guru. Baba has just made Himself present in front of me in the physical form as my Guru., my Maa. Some feelings, thoughts, experiences cannot be put on paper for lack of the right words or the words which befit the experience it takes me through. They are best seen through the tears of joy, which I have experienced reading every word in this Holy Book. I humbly surrender to the lord and thank him for having reintroduced Himself back to his disciples in this age, in this form. Thank you Baba, Thank you Jaya Maa, you have made my life worthwhile.

- Girish Chandarana
Chief Operating Officer
Media & Advertising, Bengaluru

Read Ihh Inmk hi my oplnic, this can be read once we complete the "Sal Sflclinrild". This brjit does not narrate the incidents related to Sai Babii in Shirdi, hjt with recent experiences of some people whom the author nJnew. In many places, I felt the attachment - between the Aithor & Sainath is similar to Bakhta Kanappa & Lord Shiva. 'Such a pure love, she leels, explains, narrates towards Sairam.

- Madhan
Verified Buyer
(Amazon)

It gives me great pleasure to pen these few lines about the book entitled "Sai Baba is Still Alive" by Smt. |aya Wahi. I was amazed to read the contents of the book and the various experiences of Smt)aya Wahi. As has been mentioned by Smt. Jaya Wahi in her book, verily this book "Sai Baba is Still Alive" is a modern version of the Shirdi Sai Satcharita which was written during Bhagawan Baba's time. "Sai Baba is Still Alive" is full of anecdotes, which touch the hearts of people. Each incident in the book serves to increase people's faith in Shirdi Baba. It is also intertwined with extracts taken from the original Satcharita and the parallelism between the two is quite intriguing. The wonderful thing about this book is that it is written straight from the heart without any pretention or exaggeration. One cannot help admire the depth of Smt. |aya Wahi's devotion to her beloved Lord Shirdi Baba and this comes through very clearly in this book. It also helps to reinforce the faith of existing devotees. It will be an eye opener for non-devotees who read the book. One of the reasons why the book has a very special appeal is that it is very contemporary in nature having been written just a few years ago. I have read the book several times and have no hesitation in recommending it to everyone to read.

Some of the miracles described in the book brought tears to my eyes. Indeed, I have personally collected hundreds of copies of the book and distributed it to many of my friends who have all written back to me how impressed they were with it. I do hope and pray that Ms. Jaya Wahi will bring out further editions of the book or companion volumes to the book with newer experiences of devotees, including her own personal experiences. Ms. |aya Wahi's styit of writing is very refreshing and once somebody starts reading the book, it is very difficult to put it down, as it is very gripping.

- Dr. V. Mohan

Chairman, Dr Mohan's Diabetes Specialities Centre
Awarded Padma Shri by Honourable President of India
Chennai